Food hygiene

Basic texts

Fourth edition

WORLD HEALTH ORGANIZATION

FOOD AND AGRICULTURE ORGANIZATION OF THE UNITED NATIONS

Rome, 2009

ISBN 978-92-5-105913-5

THE CODEX ALIMENTARIUS COMMISSION

The Codex Alimentarius Commission is an intergovernmental body with more than 180 members, within the framework of the Joint Food Standards Programme established by the Food and Agriculture Organization of the United Nations (FAO) and the World Health Organization (WHO), with the purpose of protecting the health of consumers and ensuring fair practices in the food trade. The Commission also promotes coordination of all food standards work undertaken by international governmental and non-governmental organizations.

The *Codex Alimentarius* (Latin, meaning Food Law or Code) is the result of the Commission's work: a collection of internationally adopted food standards, guidelines, codes of practice and other recommendations. The texts in this publication are part of the Codex Alimentarius.

FOOD HYGIENE (BASIC TEXTS)
Fourth edition

The Codex basic texts on food hygiene promote understanding of how rules and regulations on food hygiene are developed and applied. The *General Principles of food hygiene* cover hygiene practices from primary production through to final consumption, highlighting the key hygiene controls at each stage. This publication also contains the most internationally used description of the Hazard Analysis and Critical Control Point (HACCP) system and guidelines for its application. This fourth edition includes texts adopted by the Codex Alimentarius Commission up to 2009. The texts will be of use to government authorities, food industries, food handlers and consumers, as well as teachers and students of food hygiene.

Further information on these texts, or any other aspect of the Codex Alimentarius Commission, may be obtained from:

> The Secretary
> Codex Alimentarius Commission
> Joint FAO/WHO Food Standards Programme
> Viale delle Terme di Caracalla
> 00153 Rome, Italy
> Fax: +39 06 57054593
> E-mail: codex@fao.org
> http:// www.codexalimentarius.net

FOOD HYGIENE (BASIC TEXTS)
Fourth edition

CONTENTS

RECOMMENDED INTERNATIONAL CODE OF PRACTICE
GENERAL PRINCIPLES OF FOOD HYGIENE

CAC/RCP 1-1969

Adopted in 1997. Amended 1999. Revision 2003.

RECOMMENDED INTERNATIONAL CODE OF PRACTICE
GENERAL PRINCIPLES OF FOOD HYGIENE

CAC/RCP 1-1969

INTRODUCTION

People have the right to expect the food they eat to be safe and suitable for consumption. Foodborne illness and foodborne injury are at best unpleasant; at worst, they can be fatal. But there are also other consequences. Outbreaks of foodborne illness can damage trade and tourism, and lead to loss of earnings, unemployment and litigation. Food spoilage is wasteful, costly and can adversely affect trade and consumer confidence.

International food trade and foreign travel are increasing, bringing important social and economic benefits. But this also makes the spread of illness around the world easier. Eating habits too have undergone major change in many countries over the last two decades and new food production, preparation and distribution techniques have developed to reflect this. Effective hygiene control, therefore, is vital to avoid the adverse human health and economic consequences of foodborne illness, foodborne injury, and food spoilage. Everyone, including farmers and growers, manufacturers and processors, food handlers and consumers, has a responsibility to ensure that food is safe and suitable for consumption.

These General Principles lay a firm foundation for ensuring food hygiene and should be used in conjunction with each specific code of hygienic practice, where appropriate, and the guidelines on microbiological criteria. The document follows the food chain from primary production through to final consumption, highlighting the key hygiene controls at each stage. It recommends an HACCP-based approach wherever possible to enhance food safety as described in "Hazard Analysis and Critical Control Point (HACCP) system and guidelines for its application" (Annex).

The controls described in this General Principles document are internationally recognized as essential to ensure the safety and suitability of food for consumption. The General Principles are commended to Governments, industry (including individual primary producers, manufacturers, processors, food service operators and retailers) and consumers alike.

SECTION 1 – OBJECTIVES

1.1   The Codex General Principles of food hygiene:
- identify the *essential* principles of food hygiene applicable *throughout the food chain* (including primary production through to the final consumer) to achieve the goal of ensuring that food is safe and suitable for human consumption;
- recommend an HACCP-based approach as a means to enhance food safety;
- indicate *how* to implement those principles; and
- provide a *guidance* for specific codes that may be needed for sectors of the food chain, processes, or commodities to amplify the hygiene requirements specific to those areas.

SECTION 2 – SCOPE, USE AND DEFINITION

2.1   Scope

2.1.1   **The food chain**
This document follows the food chain from primary production to the final consumer, setting out the necessary hygiene conditions for producing food that is safe and suitable for consumption. The document provides a base-line structure for other, more specific, codes applicable to particular sectors. Such specific codes and guidelines should be read in conjunction with this document and "Hazard Analysis and Critical Control Point (HACCP) system and guidelines for its application" (Annex).

2.1.2   **Roles of governments, industry, and consumers**
Governments can consider the contents of this document and decide how best they should encourage the implementation of these General Principles to:
- protect consumers adequately from illness or injury caused by food; policies need to consider the vulnerability of the population, or of different groups within the population;
- provide assurance that food is suitable for human consumption;
- maintain confidence in internationally traded food; and
- provide health education programmes that effectively communicate the principles of food hygiene to industry and consumers.

Industry should apply the hygienic practices set out in this document to:
- provide food that is safe and suitable for consumption;
- ensure that consumers have clear and easily-understood information, by way of labelling and other appropriate means, to enable them to protect their food from contamination and growth/survival of foodborne pathogens by storing, handling and preparing it correctly; and
- maintain confidence in internationally traded food.

Consumers should recognize their role by following relevant instructions and applying appropriate food hygiene measures.

2.2 Use

Each section in this document states both the objectives to be achieved and the rationale behind those objectives in terms of the safety and suitability of food.

Section 3 covers primary production and associated procedures. Although hygienic practices may differ considerably for the various food commodities and specific codes should be applied where appropriate, some general guidance is given in this section. Sections 4 to 10 set down the general hygiene principles that apply throughout the food chain to the point of sale. Section 9 also covers consumer information, recognizing the important role played by consumers in maintaining the safety and suitability of food.

There will inevitably be situations where some of the specific requirements contained in this document are not applicable. The fundamental question in every case is "What is necessary and appropriate on the grounds of the safety and suitability of food for consumption?"

The text indicates where such questions are likely to arise by using the phrases "where necessary" and "where appropriate". In practice, this means that, although the requirement is generally appropriate and reasonable, there will nevertheless be some situations where it is neither necessary nor appropriate on the grounds of food safety and suitability. In deciding whether a requirement is necessary or appropriate, an assessment of the risk should be made, preferably within the framework of the HACCP approach. This approach allows the requirements in this document to be flexibly and sensibly applied with a proper regard for the overall objectives of producing food that is safe and suitable for consumption. In so doing, it takes into account the wide diversity of activities and varying degrees of risk involved in producing food. Additional guidance is available in specific food codes.

2.3 Definitions

For the purpose of this Code, the following expressions have the meaning stated:

Cleaning The removal of soil, food residue, dirt, grease or other objectionable matter.

Contaminant Any biological or chemical agent, foreign matter or other substances not intentionally added to food that may compromise food safety or suitability.

Contamination The introduction or occurrence of a contaminant in food or food environment.

Disinfection The reduction, by means of chemical agents and/or physical methods, of the number of micro-organisms in the environment to a level that does not compromise food safety or suitability.

Establishment Any building or area in which food is handled and the surroundings under the control of the same management.

Food hygiene All conditions and measures necessary to ensure the safety and suitability of food at all stages of the food chain.

Hazard A biological, chemical or physical agent in, or condition of, food with the potential to cause an adverse health effect.

HACCP A system that identifies, evaluates and controls hazards that are significant for food safety.

Food handler Any person who directly handles packaged or unpackaged food, food equipment and utensils, or food contact surfaces and is therefore expected to comply with food hygiene requirements.

Food safety Assurance that food will not cause harm to the consumer when it is prepared and/or eaten according to its intended use.

Food suitability Assurance that food is acceptable for human consumption according to its intended use.

Primary production Those steps in the food chain up to and including, for example, harvesting, slaughter, milking, fishing.

SECTION 3 – PRIMARY PRODUCTION

OBJECTIVES:
Primary production should be managed in a way that ensures that food is safe and suitable for its intended use. Where necessary, this will include:
- avoiding the use of areas where the environment poses a threat to the safety of food;
- controlling contaminants, pests and diseases of animals and plants in such a way as not to pose a threat to food safety;
- adopting practices and measures to ensure food is produced under appropriately hygienic conditions.

RATIONALE:
To reduce the likelihood of introducing a hazard that may adversely affect the safety of food, or its suitability for consumption, at later stages of the food chain.

3.1   Environmental hygiene

Potential sources of contamination from the environment should be considered. In particular, primary food production should not be carried on in areas where the presence of potentially harmful substances would lead to an unacceptable level of such substances in food.

3.2   Hygienic production of food sources

The potential effects of primary production activities on the safety and suitability of food should be considered at all times. In particular, this includes identifying any specific points in such activities where a high probability of contamination may exist and taking specific measures to minimize that probability. The HACCP-based approach may assist in the taking of such measures – see "Hazard Analysis and Critical Control Point (HACCP) system and guidelines for its application" (Annex).

Producers should as far as practicable implement measures to:

- control contamination from air, soil, water, feedstuffs, fertilizers (including natural fertilizers), pesticides, veterinary drugs or any other agent used in primary production;
- control plant and animal health so that it does not pose a threat to human health through food consumption, or adversely affect the suitability of the product; and
- protect food sources from faecal and other contamination.

In particular, care should be taken to manage wastes, and store harmful substances appropriately. On-farm programmes that achieve specific food safety goals are becoming an important part of primary production and should be encouraged.

3.3 Handling, storage and transport

Procedures should be in place to:

- sort food and food ingredients to segregate material that is evidently unfit for human consumption;
- dispose of any rejected material in a hygienic manner; and
- protect food and food ingredients from contamination by pests, or by chemical, physical or microbiological contaminants or other objectionable substances during handling, storage and transport.

Care should be taken to prevent, so far as reasonably practicable, deterioration and spoilage through appropriate measures, which may include controlling temperature, humidity, and/or other controls.

3.4 Cleaning, maintenance and personnel hygiene at primary production

Appropriate facilities and procedures should be in place to ensure that:

- any necessary cleaning and maintenance is carried out effectively; and
- an appropriate degree of personal hygiene is maintained.

SECTION 4 – ESTABLISHMENT: DESIGN AND FACILITIES

OBJECTIVES:
Depending on the nature of the operations, and the risks associated with them, premises, equipment and facilities should be located, designed and constructed to ensure that:
- contamination is minimized;
- design and layout permit appropriate maintenance, cleaning and disinfections and minimize airborne contamination;
- surfaces and materials, in particular those in contact with food, are non-toxic in intended use and, where necessary, suitably durable, and easy to maintain and clean;
- where appropriate, suitable facilities are available for temperature, humidity and other controls; and
- there is effective protection against pest access and harbourage.

RATIONALE:
Attention to good hygienic design and construction, appropriate location, and the provision of adequate facilities is necessary to enable hazards to be effectively controlled.

4.1   Location

4.1.1   Establishments
Potential sources of contamination need to be considered when deciding where to locate food establishments, as well as the effectiveness of any reasonable measures that might be taken to protect food. Establishments should not be located anywhere where, after considering such protective measures, it is clear that there will remain a threat to food safety or suitability. In particular, establishments should normally be located away from:
- environmentally polluted areas and industrial activities that pose a serious threat of contaminating food;
- areas subject to flooding unless sufficient safeguards are provided;
- areas prone to infestations of pests;
- areas where wastes, either solid or liquid, cannot be removed effectively.

4.1.2   Equipment
Equipment should be located so that it:
- permits adequate maintenance and cleaning;
- functions in accordance with its intended use; and
- facilitates good hygiene practices, including monitoring.

4.2 Premises and rooms

4.2.1 Design and layout

Where appropriate, the internal design and layout of food establishments should permit good food hygiene practices, including protection against cross-contamination between and during operations by foodstuffs.

4.2.2 Internal structures and fittings

Structures within food establishments should be soundly built of durable materials and be easy to maintain, clean and, where appropriate, able to be disinfected. In particular, the following specific conditions should be satisfied, where necessary, to protect the safety and suitability of food:

- the surfaces of walls, partitions and floors should be made of impervious materials with no toxic effect in intended use;
- walls and partitions should have a smooth surface up to a height appropriate to the operation;
- floors should be constructed to allow adequate drainage and cleaning;
- ceilings and overhead fixtures should be constructed and finished to minimize the buildup of dirt and condensation, and the shedding of particles;
- windows should be easy to clean, be constructed to minimize the buildup of dirt and, where necessary, be fitted with removable and cleanable insect-proof screens. Where necessary, windows should be fixed;
- doors should have smooth, non-absorbent surfaces, and be easy to clean and, where necessary, disinfect;
- working surfaces that come into direct contact with food should be in sound condition, durable and easy to clean, maintain and disinfect. They should be made of smooth, non-absorbent materials, and inert to the food, to detergents and disinfectants under normal operating conditions.

4.2.3 Temporary/mobile premises and vending machines

Premises and structures covered here include market stalls, mobile sales and street vending vehicles, and temporary premises in which food is handled such as tents and marquees.

Such premises and structures should be sited, designed and constructed to avoid, as far as reasonably practicable, contaminating food and harbouring pests.

In applying these specific conditions and requirements, any food hygiene hazards associated with such facilities should be adequately controlled to ensure the safety and suitability of food.

4.3 Equipment

4.3.1 General

Equipment and containers (other than once-only use containers and packaging) coming into contact with food, should be designed and constructed to ensure that, where necessary, they can be adequately cleaned, disinfected and maintained to avoid the contamination of food. Equipment and containers should be made of materials with no toxic effect in intended use. Where necessary, equipment should be durable and movable or capable of being disassembled to allow for maintenance, cleaning, disinfection, monitoring and, for example, to facilitate inspection for pests.

4.3.2 Food control and monitoring equipment

In addition to the general requirements in Section 4.3.1, equipment used to cook, heat treat, cool, store or freeze food should be designed to achieve the required food temperatures as rapidly as necessary in the interests of food safety and suitability, and maintain them effectively. Such equipment should also be designed to allow temperatures to be monitored and controlled. Where necessary, such equipment should have effective means of controlling and monitoring humidity, air-flow and any other characteristic likely to have a detrimental effect on the safety or suitability of food. These requirements are intended to ensure that:

- harmful or undesirable micro-organisms or their toxins are eliminated or reduced to safe levels or their survival and growth are effectively controlled;
- where appropriate, critical limits established in HACCP-based plans can be monitored; and
- temperatures and other conditions necessary to food safety and suitability can be rapidly achieved and maintained.

4.3.3 Containers for waste and inedible substances

Containers for waste, by-products and inedible or dangerous substances should be specifically identifiable, suitably constructed and, where appropriate, made of impervious material. Containers used to hold dangerous substances should be identified and, where appropriate, be lockable to prevent malicious or accidental contamination of food.

4.4 Facilities

4.4.1 Water supply

An adequate supply of potable water, with appropriate facilities for its storage, distribution and temperature control, should be available whenever necessary to ensure the safety and suitability of food.

Potable water should be as specified in the latest edition of *WHO Guidelines for drinking-water quality* or water of a higher standard. Non-potable water (for use in, for example, fire control, steam production, refrigeration and other similar purposes where it would not contaminate food) should have a separate system. Non-potable water systems should be identified and should not connect with, or allow reflux into, potable water systems.

4.4.2   **Drainage and waste disposal**
Adequate drainage and waste disposal systems and facilities should be provided. They should be designed and constructed so that the risk of contaminating food or the potable water supply is avoided.

4.4.3   **Cleaning**
Adequate facilities, suitably designated, should be provided for cleaning food, utensils and equipment. Such facilities should have an adequate supply of hot and cold potable water where appropriate.

4.4.4   **Personnel hygiene facilities and toilets**
Personnel hygiene facilities should be available to ensure that an appropriate degree of personal hygiene can be maintained and to avoid contaminating food. Where appropriate, facilities should include:
* adequate means of hygienically washing and drying hands, including wash basins and a supply of hot and cold (or suitably temperature controlled) water;
* lavatories of appropriate hygienic design; and
* adequate changing facilities for personnel.

Such facilities should be suitably located and designated.

4.4.5   **Temperature control**
Depending on the nature of the food operations undertaken, adequate facilities should be available for heating, cooling, cooking, refrigerating and freezing food, for storing refrigerated or frozen foods, monitoring food temperatures, and, when necessary, controlling ambient temperatures to ensure the safety and suitability of food.

4.4.6   **Air quality and ventilation**
Adequate means of natural or mechanical ventilation should be provided, in particular to:
* minimize airborne contamination of food, for example, from aerosols and condensation droplets;
* control ambient temperatures;
* control odours that might affect the suitability of food; and
* control humidity, where necessary, to ensure the safety and suitability of food.

Ventilation systems should be designed and constructed so that air does not flow from contaminated areas to clean areas and, where necessary, they can be adequately maintained and cleaned.

4.4.7   **Lighting**
Adequate natural or artificial lighting should be provided to enable the undertaking to operate in a hygienic manner. Where necessary, lighting should not be such that the resulting colour is misleading. The intensity should be adequate to the nature of the

operation. Lighting fixtures should, where appropriate, be protected to ensure that food is not contaminated by breakages.

4.4.8   Storage

Where necessary, adequate facilities for the storage of food, ingredients and non-food chemicals (e.g. cleaning materials, lubricants, fuels) should be provided.

Where appropriate, food storage facilities should be designed and constructed to:
- permit adequate maintenance and cleaning;
- avoid pest access and harbourage;
- enable food to be effectively protected from contamination during storage; and
- where necessary, provide an environment that minimizes the deterioration of food (e.g. by temperature and humidity control).

The type of storage facilities required will depend on the nature of the food. Where necessary, separate, secure storage facilities for cleaning materials and hazardous substances should be provided.

SECTION 5 – CONTROL OF OPERATION

OBJECTIVE:
To produce food that is safe and suitable for human consumption by:
- formulating design requirements with respect to raw materials, composition, processing, distribution and consumer use to be met in the manufacture and handling of specific food items; and
- designing, implementing, monitoring and reviewing effective control systems.

RATIONALE:
To reduce the risk of unsafe food by taking preventive measures to ensure the safety and suitability of food at an appropriate stage in the operation by controlling food hazards.

5.1   Control of food hazards

Food business operators should control food hazards through the use of systems such as HACCP. They should:
- *identify* any steps in their operations that are critical to the safety of food;
- *implement* effective control procedures at those steps;
- *monitor* control procedures to ensure their continuing effectiveness; and
- *review* control procedures periodically, and whenever the operations change.

These systems should be applied throughout the food chain to control food hygiene throughout the shelf-life of the product through proper product and process design.

Control procedures may be simple, such as checking stock rotation, calibrating equipment or correctly loading refrigerated display units. In some cases, a system based on expert advice, and involving documentation, may be appropriate. A model of such a food safety system is described in "Hazard Analysis and Critical Control Point (HACCP) system and guidelines for its application" (Annex).

5.2 Key aspects of hygiene control systems

5.2.1 Time and temperature control

Inadequate food temperature control is one of the most common causes of foodborne illness or food spoilage. Such controls include time and temperature of cooking, cooling, processing and storage. Systems should be in place to ensure that temperature is controlled effectively where it is critical to the safety and suitability of food.

Temperature control systems should take into account:
- the nature of the food, e.g. its water activity, pH, and likely initial level and types of micro-organisms;
- the intended shelf-life of the product;
- the method of packaging and processing; and
- how the product is intended to be used, e.g. further cooking/processing or ready-to-eat.

Such systems should also specify tolerable limits for time and temperature variations.

Temperature recording devices should be checked at regular intervals and tested for accuracy.

5.2.2 Specific process steps

Other steps that contribute to food hygiene may include, for example:
- chilling,
- thermal processing,
- irradiation,
- drying,
- chemical preservation,
- vacuum or modified atmospheric packaging.

5.2.3 Microbiological and other specifications

Management systems described in Section 5.1 offer an effective way of ensuring the safety and suitability of food. Where microbiological, chemical or physical specifications are used in any food control system, such specifications should be based on sound scientific principles and state, where appropriate, monitoring procedures, analytical methods and action limits.

5.2.4 Microbiological cross-contamination

Pathogens can be transferred from one food to another, either by direct contact or by food handlers, contact surfaces or the air. Raw, unprocessed food should be effectively separated, either physically or by time, from ready-to-eat foods, with effective intermediate cleaning and, where appropriate, disinfection.

Access to processing areas may need to be restricted or controlled. Where risks are particularly high, access to processing areas should be only via a changing facility. Personnel may need to be required to put on clean protective clothing, including footwear, and wash their hands before entering.

Surfaces, utensils, equipment, fixtures and fittings should be thoroughly cleaned and, where necessary, disinfected after raw food, particularly meat and poultry, has been handled or processed.

5.2.5 **Physical and chemical contamination**
Systems should be in place to prevent contamination of foods by foreign bodies such as glass or metal shards from machinery, dust, harmful fumes and unwanted chemicals. In manufacturing and processing, suitable detection or screening devices should be used where necessary.

5.3 Incoming material requirements
No raw material or ingredient should be accepted by an establishment if it is known to contain parasites, undesirable micro-organisms, pesticides, veterinary drugs or toxic, decomposed or extraneous substances that would not be reduced to an acceptable level by normal sorting and/or processing. Where appropriate, specifications for raw materials should be identified and applied.

Raw materials or ingredients should, where appropriate, be inspected and sorted before processing. Where necessary, laboratory tests should be made to establish fitness for use. Only sound, suitable raw materials or ingredients should be used.

Stocks of raw materials and ingredients should be subject to effective stock rotation.

5.4 Packaging
Packaging design and materials should provide adequate protection for products to minimize contamination, prevent damage and accommodate proper labelling. Packaging materials or gases where used must be non-toxic and not pose a threat to the safety and suitability of food under the specified conditions of storage and use. Where appropriate, reusable packaging should be suitably durable, easy to clean and, where necessary, disinfect.

5.5 Water

5.5.1 **In contact with food**
Only potable water should be used in food handling and processing, with the following exceptions:
- for steam production, fire control and other similar purposes not connected with food; and

- in certain food processes, e.g. chilling, and in food handling areas, provided this does not constitute a hazard to the safety and suitability of food (e.g. the use of clean seawater).

Water recirculated for reuse should be treated and maintained in such a condition that no risk to the safety and suitability of food results from its use. The treatment process should be effectively monitored. Recirculated water that has received no further treatment and water recovered from processing of food by evaporation or drying may be used, provided its use does not constitute a risk to the safety and suitability of food.

5.5.2   **As an ingredient**
Potable water should be used wherever necessary to avoid food contamination.

5.5.3   **Ice and steam**
Ice should be made from water that complies with Section 4.4.1. Ice and steam should be produced, handled and stored to protect them from contamination.

Steam used in direct contact with food or food contact surfaces should not constitute a threat to the safety and suitability of food.

5.6   Management and supervision
The type of control and supervision needed will depend on the size of the business, the nature of its activities and the types of food involved. Managers and supervisors should have enough knowledge of food hygiene principles and practices to be able to judge potential risks, take appropriate preventive and corrective action, and ensure that effective monitoring and supervision takes place.

5.7   Documentation and records
Where necessary, appropriate records of processing, production and distribution should be kept and retained for a period that exceeds the shelf-life of the product. Documentation can enhance the credibility and effectiveness of the food safety control system.

5.8   Recall procedures
Managers should ensure effective procedures are in place to deal with any food safety hazard and to enable the complete, rapid recall of any implicated lot of the finished food from the market. Where a product has been withdrawn because of an immediate health hazard, other products that are produced under similar conditions, and which may present a similar hazard to public health, should be evaluated for safety and may need to be withdrawn. The need for public warnings should be considered.

Recalled products should be held under supervision until they are destroyed, used for purposes other than human consumption, determined to be safe for human consumption, or reprocessed in a manner to ensure their safety.

SECTION 6 – ESTABLISHMENT: MAINTENANCE AND SANITATION

OBJECTIVE:
To establish effective systems to:
- ensure adequate and appropriate maintenance and cleaning;
- control pests;
- manage waste; and
- monitor effectiveness of maintenance and sanitation procedures.

RATIONALE:
To facilitate the continuing effective control of food hazards, pests and other agents likely to contaminate food.

6.1 Maintenance and cleaning

6.1.1 General

Establishments and equipment should be kept in an appropriate state of repair and condition to:
- facilitate all sanitation procedures;
- function as intended, particularly at critical steps (see Section 5.1);
- prevent contamination of food, e.g. from metal shards, flaking plaster, debris and chemicals.

Cleaning should remove food residues and dirt that may be a source of contamination. The necessary cleaning methods and materials will depend on the nature of the food business. Disinfection may be necessary after cleaning.

Cleaning chemicals should be handled and used carefully and in accordance with manufacturers' instructions and stored, where necessary, separated from food, in clearly identified containers to avoid the risk of contaminating food.

6.1.2 Cleaning procedures and methods

Cleaning can be carried out by the separate or the combined use of physical methods, such as heat, scrubbing, turbulent flow, vacuum cleaning or other methods that avoid the use of water, and chemical methods using detergents, alkalis or acids.

Cleaning procedures will involve, where appropriate:
- removing gross debris from surfaces;
- applying a detergent solution to loosen soil and bacterial film and hold them in solution or suspension;
- rinsing with water that complies with Section 4 to remove loosened soil and residues of detergent;
- dry cleaning or other appropriate methods for removing and collecting residues and debris; and

- where necessary, disinfection with subsequent rinsing unless the manufacturers' instructions indicate on scientific basis that rinsing is not required.

6.2 Cleaning programmes

Cleaning and disinfection programmes should ensure that all parts of the establishment are appropriately clean, and should include the cleaning of cleaning equipment.

Cleaning and disinfection programmes should be continually and effectively monitored for their suitability and effectiveness and, where necessary, documented.

Where written cleaning programmes are used, they should specify:
- areas, items of equipment and utensils to be cleaned;
- responsibility for particular tasks;
- method and frequency of cleaning; and
- monitoring arrangements.

Where appropriate, programmes should be drawn up in consultation with relevant specialist expert advisors.

6.3 Pest control systems

6.3.1 General

Pests pose a major threat to the safety and suitability of food. Pest infestations can occur where there are breeding sites and a supply of food. Good hygiene practices should be employed to avoid creating an environment conducive to pests. Good sanitation, inspection of incoming materials and good monitoring can minimize the likelihood of infestation and thereby limit the need for pesticides.

6.3.2 Preventing access

Buildings should be kept in good repair and condition to prevent pest access and to eliminate potential breeding sites. Holes, drains and other places where pests are likely to gain access should be kept sealed. Wire mesh screens, for example on open windows, doors and ventilators, will reduce the problem of pest entry. Animals should, wherever possible, be excluded from the grounds of factories and food processing plants.

6.3.3 Harbourage and infestation

The availability of food and water encourages pest harbourage and infestation. Potential food sources should be stored in pest-proof containers and/or stacked above the ground and away from walls. Areas both inside and outside food premises should be kept clean. Where appropriate, refuse should be stored in covered, pest-proof containers.

6.3.4 Monitoring and detection

Establishments and surrounding areas should be regularly examined for evidence of infestation.

6.3.5 **Eradication**

Pest infestations should be dealt with immediately and without adversely affecting food safety or suitability. Treatment with chemical, physical or biological agents should be carried out without posing a threat to the safety or suitability of food.

6.4 Waste management

Suitable provision must be made for the removal and storage of waste. Waste must not be allowed to accumulate in food handling, food storage and other working areas and the adjoining environment except so far as is unavoidable for the proper functioning of the business.

Waste stores must be kept appropriately clean.

6.5 Monitoring effectiveness

Sanitation systems should be monitored for effectiveness, periodically verified by means such as audit pre-operational inspections or, where appropriate, microbiological sampling of environment and food contact surfaces, and regularly reviewed and adapted to reflect changed circumstances.

SECTION 7 – ESTABLISHMENT: PERSONAL HYGIENE

OBJECTIVES:
To ensure that those who come directly or indirectly into contact with food are not likely to contaminate food by:
- maintaining an appropriate degree of personal cleanliness;
- behaving and operating in an appropriate manner.

RATIONALE:
People who do not maintain an appropriate degree of personal cleanliness, who have certain illnesses or conditions or who behave inappropriately can contaminate food and transmit illness to consumers.

7.1 Health status

People known, or suspected, to be suffering from, or to be a carrier of, a disease or illness likely to be transmitted through food should not be allowed to enter any food handling area if there is a likelihood of their contaminating food. Any person so affected should immediately report illness or symptoms of illness to the management.

Medical examination of a food handler should be carried out if clinically or epidemiologically indicated.

7.2   Illness and injuries
Conditions that should be reported to management so that any need for medical examination and/or possible exclusion from food handling can be considered include:

- jaundice;
- diarrhoea;
- vomiting;
- fever;
- sore throat with fever;
- visibly infected skin lesions (boils, cuts, etc.);
- discharges from the ear, eye or nose.

7.3   Personal cleanliness
Food handlers should maintain a high degree of personal cleanliness and, where appropriate, wear suitable protective clothing, head covering and footwear. Cuts and wounds, where personnel are permitted to continue working, should be covered by suitable waterproof dressings.

Personnel should always wash their hands when personal cleanliness may affect food safety, for example:

- at the start of food handling activities;
- immediately after using the toilet; and
- after handling raw food or any contaminated material where this could result in contamination of other food items; they should avoid handling ready-to-eat food, where appropriate.

7.4   Personal behaviour
People engaged in food handling activities should refrain from behaviour that could result in contamination of food, for example:

- smoking;
- spitting;
- chewing or eating;
- sneezing or coughing over unprotected food.

Personal effects such as jewellery, watches, pins or other items should not be worn or brought into food handling areas if they pose a threat to the safety and suitability of food.

7.5   Visitors
Visitors to food manufacturing, processing or handling areas should, where appropriate, wear protective clothing and adhere to the other personal hygiene provisions in this section.

SECTION 8 – TRANSPORTATION

OBJECTIVES:

Measures should be taken where necessary to:

- protect food from potential sources of contamination;
- protect food from damage likely to render the food unsuitable for consumption; and
- provide an environment that effectively controls the growth of pathogenic or spoilage micro-organisms and the production of toxins in food.

RATIONALE:

Food may become contaminated, or may not reach its destination in a suitable condition for consumption, unless effective control measures are taken during transport, even where adequate hygiene control measures have been taken earlier in the food chain.

8.1   General

Food must be adequately protected during transport. The type of conveyances or containers required depends on the nature of the food and the conditions under which it has to be transported.

8.2   Requirements

Where necessary, conveyances and bulk containers should be designed and constructed so that they:

- do not contaminate foods or packaging;
- can be effectively cleaned and, where necessary, disinfected;
- permit effective separation of different foods or foods from non-food items where necessary during transport;
- provide effective protection from contamination, including dust and fumes;
- can effectively maintain the temperature, humidity, atmosphere and other conditions necessary to protect food from harmful or undesirable microbial growth and deterioration likely to render it unsuitable for consumption; and
- allow any necessary temperature, humidity and other conditions to be checked.

8.3   Use and maintenance

Conveyances and containers for transporting food should be kept in an appropriate state of cleanliness, repair and condition. Where the same conveyance or container is used for transporting different foods, or non-foods, effective cleaning and, where necessary, disinfection should take place between loads.

Where appropriate, particularly in bulk transport, containers and conveyances should be designated and marked for food use only and be used only for that purpose.

SECTION 9 – PRODUCT INFORMATION AND CONSUMER AWARENESS

OBJECTIVES:
Products should bear appropriate information to ensure that:
- adequate and accessible information is available to the next person in the food chain to enable them to handle, store, process, prepare and display the product safely and correctly;
- the lot or batch can be easily identified and recalled if necessary.

Consumers should have enough knowledge of food hygiene to enable them to:
- understand the importance of product information;
- make informed choices appropriate to the individual; and
- prevent contamination and growth or survival of foodborne pathogens by storing, preparing and using it correctly.

Information for industry or trade users should be clearly distinguishable from consumer information, particularly on food labels.

RATIONALE:
Insufficient product information and/or inadequate knowledge of general food hygiene can lead to products being mishandled at later stages in the food chain. Such mishandling can result in illness or products becoming unsuitable for consumption, even where adequate hygiene control measures have been taken earlier in the food chain.

9.1 Lot identification

Lot identification is essential in product recall and also helps effective stock rotation. Each container of food should be permanently marked to identify the producer and the lot. *General Standard for the labelling of prepackaged foods* (CODEX STAN 1-1985) applies.

9.2 Product information

All food products should be accompanied by or bear adequate information to enable the next person in the food chain to handle, display, store and prepare and use the product safely and correctly.

9.3 Labelling

Prepackaged foods should be labelled with clear instructions to enable the next person in the food chain to handle, display, store and use the product safely. *General Standard for the labelling of prepackaged foods* (CODEX STAN 1-1985) applies.

9.4 Consumer education

Health education programmes should cover general food hygiene. Such programmes should enable consumers to understand the importance of any product information, follow any instructions accompanying products, and make informed choices. In particular, consumers should be informed of the relationship between time/temperature control and foodborne illness.

SECTION 10 – TRAINING

OBJECTIVE:
Those engaged in food operations who come directly or indirectly into contact with food should be trained and/or instructed in food hygiene to a level appropriate to the operations they are to perform.
RATIONALE:
Training is fundamentally important to any food hygiene system. Inadequate hygiene training and/or instruction and supervision of *all* people involved in food related activities pose a potential threat to the safety of food and its suitability for consumption.

10.1 Awareness and responsibilities

Food hygiene training is fundamentally important. All personnel should be aware of their role and responsibility in protecting food from contamination or deterioration. Food handlers should have the necessary knowledge and skills to enable them to handle food hygienically. Those who handle strong cleaning chemicals or other potentially hazardous chemicals should be instructed in safe handling techniques.

10.2 Training programmes

Factors to take into account in assessing the level of training required include:
- the nature of the food, in particular its ability to sustain growth of pathogenic or spoilage micro-organisms;
- the manner in which the food is handled and packed, including the probability of contamination;
- the extent and nature of processing or further preparation before final consumption;
- the conditions under which the food will be stored; and
- the expected length of time before consumption.

10.3 Instruction and supervision

Periodic assessments of the effectiveness of training and instruction programmes should be made, as well as routine supervision and checks to ensure that procedures are being carried out effectively.

Managers and supervisors of food processes should have the necessary knowledge of food hygiene principles and practices to be able to judge potential risks and take the necessary action to remedy deficiencies.

10.4 Refresher training

Training programmes should be routinely reviewed and updated where necessary. Systems should be in place to ensure that food handlers remain aware of all procedures necessary to maintain the safety and suitability of food.

HAZARD ANALYSIS AND CRITICAL CONTROL POINT (HACCP) SYSTEM AND GUIDELINES FOR ITS APPLICATION

Annex to CAC/RCP 1-1969

PREAMBLE

The first section of this document sets out the principles of the Hazard Analysis and Critical Control Point (HACCP) system adopted by the Codex Alimentarius Commission. The second section provides general guidance for the application of the system while recognizing that the details of application may vary depending on the circumstances of the food operation.[1]

The HACCP system, which is science-based and systematic, identifies specific hazards and measures for their control to ensure the safety of food. HACCP is a tool to assess hazards and establish control systems that focus on prevention rather than relying mainly on end-product testing. Any HACCP system is capable of accommodating change, such as advances in equipment design, processing procedures or technological developments.

HACCP can be applied throughout the food chain from primary production to final consumption and its implementation should be guided by scientific evidence of risks to human health. As well as enhancing food safety, implementation of HACCP can provide other significant benefits. In addition, the application of HACCP systems can aid inspection by regulatory authorities and promote international trade by increasing confidence in food safety.

The successful application of HACCP requires the full commitment and involvement of management and the workforce. It also requires a multidisciplinary approach; this multidisciplinary approach should include, where appropriate, expertise in agronomy, veterinary health, production, microbiology, medicine, public health, food technology, environmental health, chemistry and engineering, according to the particular study. The application of HACCP is compatible with the implementation of quality management systems, such as the ISO 9000 series, and is the system of choice in the management of food safety within such systems.

While the application of HACCP to food safety is considered here, the concept can be applied to other aspects of food quality.

---

[1] The principles of the HACCP system set the basis for the requirements for the application of HACCP, while the guidelines for the application provide general guidance for practical application.

DEFINITIONS

Control (verb) To take all necessary actions to ensure and maintain compliance with criteria established in the HACCP plan.

Control (noun) The state wherein correct procedures are being followed and criteria are being met.

Control measure Any action and activity that can be used to prevent or eliminate a food safety hazard or reduce it to an acceptable level.

Corrective action Any action to be taken when the results of monitoring at the CCP indicate a loss of control.

Critical Control Point (CCP) A step at which control can be applied and is essential to prevent or eliminate a food safety hazard or reduce it to an acceptable level.

Critical limit A criterion that separates acceptability from unacceptability.

Deviation Failure to meet a critical limit.

Flow diagram A systematic representation of the sequence of steps or operations used in the production or manufacture of a particular food item.

HACCP A system that identifies, evaluates and controls hazards that are significant for food safety.

HACCP plan A document prepared in accordance with the principles of HACCP to ensure control of hazards that are significant for food safety in the segment of the food chain under consideration.

Hazard A biological, chemical or physical agent in, or condition of, food with the potential to cause an adverse health effect.

Hazard analysis The process of collecting and evaluating information on hazards and conditions leading to their presence to decide which are significant for food safety and therefore should be addressed in the HACCP plan.

Monitoring The act of conducting a planned sequence of observations or measurements of control parameters to assess whether a CCP is under control.

Step A point, procedure, operation or stage in the food chain, including raw materials, from primary production to final consumption.

Validation Obtaining evidence that the elements of the HACCP plan are effective.

Verification The application of methods, procedures, tests and other evaluations, in addition to monitoring, to determine compliance with the HACCP plan.

PRINCIPLES OF THE HACCP SYSTEM

The HACCP system consists of the following seven principles:

PRINCIPLE 1
Conduct a hazard analysis.

PRINCIPLE 2
Determine the Critical Control Points (CCPs).

PRINCIPLE 3
Establish critical limit(s).

PRINCIPLE 4
Establish a system to monitor control of the CCP.

PRINCIPLE 5
Establish the corrective action to be taken when monitoring indicates that a particular CCP is not under control.

PRINCIPLE 6
Establish procedures for verification to confirm that the HACCP system is working effectively.

PRINCIPLE 7
Establish documentation concerning all procedures and records appropriate to these principles and their application.

GUIDELINES FOR THE APPLICATION OF THE HACCP SYSTEM

INTRODUCTION
Prior to application of HACCP to any sector of the food chain, that sector should have in place prerequisite programmes such as good hygienic practices according to the *Recommended International Code of Practice – General Principles of food hygiene*, the appropriate Codex Codes of practice, and appropriate food safety requirements. These prerequisite programmes to HACCP, including training, should be well established, fully operational and verified in order to facilitate the successful application and implementation of the HACCP system.

For all types of food business, management awareness and commitment is necessary for implementation of an effective HACCP system. The effectiveness will also rely upon management and employees having the appropriate HACCP knowledge and skills.

During hazard identification, evaluation and subsequent operations in designing and applying HACCP systems, consideration must be given to the impact of raw materials, ingredients, food manufacturing practices, role of manufacturing processes to control hazards, likely end use of the product, categories of consumers of concern, and epidemiological evidence relative to food safety.

The intent of the HACCP system is to focus control at CCPs. Redesign of the operation should be considered if a hazard that must be controlled is identified but no CCPs are found.

HACCP should be applied to each specific operation separately. CCPs identified in any given example in any Codex Code of hygienic practice might not be the only ones identified for a specific application or might be of a different nature. The HACCP application should be reviewed and necessary changes made when any modification is made in the product, process or any step.

The application of the HACCP principles should be the responsibility of each individual business. However, it is recognized by governments and businesses that there may be obstacles that hinder the effective application of the HACCP principles by individual businesses. This is particularly relevant in small and/or less-developed businesses. While it is recognized that, when applying HACCP, flexibility appropriate to the business is important, all seven principles must be applied in the HACCP system. This flexibility should take into account the nature and size of the operation, including the human and financial resources, infrastructure, processes, knowledge and practical constraints.

Small and/or less-developed businesses do not always have the resources and the necessary expertise on-site for the development and implementation of an effective HACCP plan. In such situations, expert advice should be obtained from other sources, which may include: trade and industry associations, independent experts and regulatory authorities. HACCP literature and especially sector-specific HACCP guides can be valuable. HACCP guidance developed by experts relevant to the process or type of operation may provide a useful tool for businesses in designing and implementing the HACCP plan. Where businesses are using expertly developed HACCP guidance, it is essential that it is specific to the foods and/or processes under consideration. More detailed information on the obstacles in implementing HACCP, particularly in reference to small and/or less-developed businesses, and recommendations in resolving these obstacles, can be found in *Obstacles to the application of HACCP, particularly in small and less-developed businesses, and approaches to overcome them* (document in preparation by FAO/WHO).

The efficacy of any HACCP system will nevertheless rely on management and employees having the appropriate HACCP knowledge and skills. Therefore, ongoing training is necessary for all levels of employees and managers, as appropriate.

APPLICATION
The application of HACCP principles consists of the following tasks as identified in the Logic Sequence for Application of HACCP (Figure 1).

1. Assemble HACCP team
The food operation should ensure that the appropriate product-specific knowledge and expertise is available for the development of an effective HACCP plan. Optimally, this may be accomplished by assembling a multidisciplinary team. Where such expertise is not available on-site, expert advice should be obtained from other sources, such as trade and industry associations, independent experts, regulatory authorities, HACCP literature and HACCP guidance (including sector-specific HACCP guides). It may be possible that a well-trained individual with access to such guidance is able to implement HACCP in-house. The scope of the HACCP plan should be identified. The scope should describe which segment of the food chain is involved and the general classes of hazards to be addressed (e.g. Does it cover all classes of hazards or only selected classes?).

2. Describe product

A full description of the product should be drawn up, including relevant safety information such as: composition, physical/chemical structure (including A_w, pH, etc.), microcidal/static treatments (heat-treatment, freezing, brining, smoking, etc.), packaging, durability, storage conditions and method of distribution. Within businesses with multiple products, for example, catering operations, it may be effective to group products with similar characteristics or processing steps for the purpose of development of the HACCP plan.

3. Identify intended use

The intended use should be based on the expected uses of the product by the end user or consumer. In specific cases, vulnerable groups of the population, e.g. institutional feeding, may have to be considered.

4. Construct flow diagram

The flow diagram should be constructed by the HACCP team (see also "Assemble HACCP team" above). The flow diagram should cover all steps in the operation for a specific product. The same flow diagram may be used for a number of products that are manufactured using similar processing steps. When applying HACCP to a given operation, consideration should be given to steps preceding and following the specified operation.

5. On-site confirmation of flow diagram

Steps must be taken to confirm the processing operation against the flow diagram during all stages and hours of operation and amend the flow diagram where appropriate. The confirmation of the flow diagram should be performed by a person or persons with sufficient knowledge of the processing operation.

6. List all potential hazards associated with each step, conduct a hazard analysis, and consider any measures to control identified hazards
(see Principle 1)

The HACCP team (see "assemble HACCP team" above) should list all of the hazards that may be reasonably expected to occur at each step according to the scope from primary production, processing, manufacture and distribution until the point of consumption.

The HACCP team (see "assemble HACCP team") should next conduct a hazard analysis to identify for the HACCP plan which hazards are of such a nature that their elimination or reduction to acceptable levels is essential to the production of a safe food.

In conducting the hazard analysis, wherever possible, the following should be included:
- the likely occurrence of hazards and severity of their adverse health effects;
- the qualitative and/or quantitative evaluation of the presence of hazards;
- survival or multiplication of micro-organisms of concern;
- production or persistence in foods of toxins, chemicals or physical agents; and
- conditions leading to the above.

Consideration should be given to what control measures, if any exist, can be applied to each hazard.

More than one control measure may be required to control a specific hazard(s) and more than one hazard may be controlled by a specified control measure.

7. Determine CCPs
(see Principle 2)[2]

There may be more than one CCP at which control is applied to address the same hazard. The determination of a CCP in the HACCP system can be facilitated by the application of a decision tree (e.g. Figure 2), which indicates a logic reasoning approach. Application of a decision tree should be flexible, given whether the operation is for production, slaughter, processing, storage, distribution or other. It should be used for guidance when determining CCPs. This example of a decision tree may not be applicable to all situations. Other approaches may be used. Training in the application of the decision tree is recommended.

If a hazard has been identified at a step where control is necessary for safety, and no control measure exists at that step, or any other, then the product or process should be modified at that step, or at any earlier or later stage, to include a control measure.

8. Establish critical limits for each CCP
(see Principle 3)

Critical limits must be specified and validated for each CCP. In some cases, more than one critical limit will be elaborated at a particular step. Criteria often used include measurements of temperature, time, moisture level, pH, A_w, available chlorine, and sensory parameters such as visual appearance and texture.

Where HACCP guidance developed by experts has been used to establish the critical limits, care should be taken to ensure that these limits fully apply to the specific operation, product or groups of products under consideration. These critical limits should be measurable.

9. Establish a monitoring system for each CCP
(see Principle 4)

Monitoring is the scheduled measurement or observation of a CCP relative to its critical limits. The monitoring procedures must be able to detect loss of control at the CCP. Further, monitoring should ideally provide this information in time to make adjustments to ensure control of the process to prevent violating the critical limits. Where possible, process adjustments should be made when monitoring results indicate a trend towards loss of control at a CCP. The adjustments should be taken before a deviation occurs. Data derived from monitoring must be evaluated by a designated

---

[2] Since the publication of the decision tree by Codex, its use has been implemented many times for training purposes. In many instances, while this tree has been useful to explain the logic and depth of understanding needed to determine CCPs, it is not specific to all food operations, e.g. slaughter, and therefore it should be used in conjunction with professional judgement, and modified in some cases.

person with knowledge and authority to carry out corrective actions when indicated. If monitoring is not continuous, then the amount or frequency of monitoring must be sufficient to guarantee the CCP is in control. Most monitoring procedures for CCPs will need to be done rapidly because they relate to online processes and there will not be time for lengthy analytical testing. Physical and chemical measurements are often preferred to microbiological testing because they may be done rapidly and can often indicate the microbiological control of the product.

All records and documents associated with monitoring CCPs must be signed by the person(s) doing the monitoring and by a responsible reviewing official(s) of the company.

10. Establish corrective actions
(see Principle 5)
Specific corrective actions must be developed for each CCP in the HACCP system in order to deal with deviations when they occur.

The actions must ensure that the CCP has been brought under control. Actions taken must also include proper disposition of the affected product. Deviation and product disposition procedures must be documented in the HACCP record-keeping.

11. Establish verification procedures
(see Principle 6)
Establish procedures for verification. Verification and auditing methods, procedures and tests, including random sampling and analysis, can be used to determine if the HACCP system is working correctly. The frequency of verification should be sufficient to confirm that the HACCP system is working effectively.

Verification should be carried out by someone other than the person who is responsible for performing the monitoring and corrective actions. Where certain verification activities cannot be performed in-house, verification should be performed on behalf of the business by external experts or qualified third parties.

Examples of verification activities include:
- review of the HACCP system and plan and its records;
- review of deviations and product dispositions;
- confirmation that CCPs are kept under control.

Where possible, validation activities should include actions to confirm the efficacy of all elements of the HACCP system.

12. Establish documentation and record-keeping
(see Principle 7)
Efficient and accurate record-keeping is essential to the application of an HACCP system. HACCP procedures should be documented. Documentation and record-keeping should be appropriate to the nature and size of the operation and sufficient to assist

the business to verify that the HACCP controls are in place and being maintained. Expertly developed HACCP guidance materials (e.g. sector-specific HACCP guides) may be utilized as part of the documentation, provided that those materials reflect the specific food operations of the business.

Documentation examples are:
- hazard analysis;
- CCP determination;
- critical limit determination.

Record examples are:
- CCP monitoring activities;
- deviations and associated corrective actions;
- verification procedures performed;
- modifications to the HACCP plan;

An example of an HACCP worksheet for the development of an HACCP plan is attached as Figure 3.

A simple record-keeping system can be effective and easily communicated to employees. It may be integrated into existing operations and may use existing paperwork, such as delivery invoices and checklists, to record, for example, product temperatures.

TRAINING

Training of personnel in industry, government and academia in HACCP principles and applications and increasing awareness of consumers are essential elements for the effective implementation of HACCP. As an aid in developing specific training to support an HACCP plan, working instructions and procedures should be developed that define the tasks of the operating personnel to be stationed at each CCP.

Cooperation between primary producer, industry, trade groups, consumer organizations, and responsible authorities is of vital importance. Opportunities should be provided for the joint training of industry and control authorities to encourage and maintain a continuous dialogue and create a climate of understanding in the practical application of HACCP.

Figure 1
Logic sequence for application of HACCP

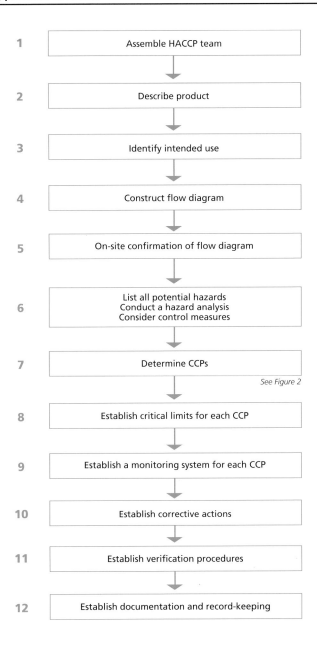

Figure 2
Example of decision tree to identify CCPs

(Answer questions in sequence)

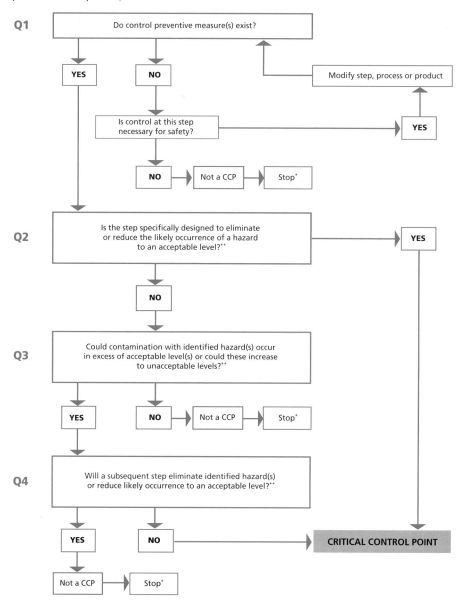

* Proceed to the next identified hazard in the described process.
** Acceptable and unacceptable levels need to be defined within the overall objectives in identifying the CCPs of HACCP plan.

Figure 3
Example of an HACCP worksheet

1 | Describe product |

2 | Diagram process flow |

3

LIST							
Step	Hazard(s)	Control measure(s)	CCPs	Critical limit(s)	Monitoring procedure(s)	Corrective action(s)	Record(s)

4 | Verification |

PRINCIPLES FOR THE ESTABLISHMENT AND APPLICATION OF MICROBIOLOGICAL CRITERIA FOR FOODS

CAC/GL 21-1997

PRINCIPLES FOR THE ESTABLISHMENT AND APPLICATION OF MICROBIOLOGICAL CRITERIA FOR FOODS

CAC/GL 21-1997

INTRODUCTION

These Principles are intended to give guidance on the establishment and application of microbiological criteria for foods at any point in the food chain from primary production to final consumption.

The safety of foods is principally ensured by control at the source, product design and process control, and the application of good hygienic practices during production, processing (including labelling), handling, distribution, storage, sale, preparation and use, in conjunction with the application of the HACCP system. This preventive approach offers more control than microbiological testing because the effectiveness of microbiological examination to assess the safety of foods is limited. Guidance for the establishment of HACCP-based systems is detailed in "Hazard Analysis and Critical Control Point (HACCP) system and guidelines for its application" (Annex to *Recommended International Code of Practice – General Principles of food hygiene* [CAC/RCP 1-1969]).

Microbiological criteria should be established according to these principles and be based on scientific analysis and advice, and, where sufficient data are available, a risk analysis appropriate to the foodstuff and its use. Microbiological criteria should be developed in a transparent fashion and meet the requirements of fair trade. They should be reviewed periodically for relevance with respect to emerging pathogens, changing technologies, and new understandings of science.

1. DEFINITION OF MICROBIOLOGICAL CRITERION

A microbiological criterion for food defines the acceptability of a product or a food lot based on the absence or presence or number of micro-organisms including parasites, and/or quantity of their toxins/metabolites, per unit(s) of mass, volume, area or lot.

2. COMPONENTS OF MICROBIOLOGICAL CRITERIA FOR FOODS

2.1   A microbiological criterion consists of:
   * a statement of the micro-organisms of concern and/or their toxins/metabolites and the reason for that concern (see Section 5.1);
   * the analytical methods for their detection and/or quantification (see Section 5.2);
   * a plan defining the number of field samples to be taken and the size of the analytical unit (see Section 6);
   * microbiological limits considered appropriate to the food at the specified point(s) of the food chain (see Section 5.3);
   * the number of analytical units that should conform to these limits.

2.2   A microbiological criterion should also state:
- the food to which the criterion applies;
- the point(s) in the food chain where the criterion applies; and
- any actions to be taken when the criterion is not met.

2.3   When applying a microbiological criterion for assessing products, it is essential, in order to make the best use of money and personnel, that only appropriate tests be applied (see Section 5) to those foods and at those points in the food chain that offer maximum benefit in providing the consumer with a food that is safe and suitable for consumption.

3. PURPOSES AND APPLICATION OF MICROBIOLOGICAL CRITERIA FOR FOODS

3.1   Microbiological criteria may be used to formulate design requirements and to indicate the required microbiological status of raw materials, ingredients and end products at any stage of the food chain as appropriate. They may be relevant to the examination of foods, including raw materials and ingredients, of unknown or uncertain origin or when other means of verifying the efficacy of HACCP-based systems and good hygienic practices are not available. Generally, microbiological criteria may be applied to define the distinction between acceptable and unacceptable raw materials, ingredients, products and lots by regulatory authorities and/or food business operators. Microbiological criteria may also be used to determine that processes are consistent with the *Recommended International Code of Practice – General Principles of food hygiene* (CAC/RCP 1-1969).

3.1.1   Application by regulatory authorities
Microbiological criteria can be used to define and check compliance with the microbiological requirements.

Mandatory microbiological criteria shall apply to those products and/or points of the food chain where no other more effective tools are available, and where they are expected to improve the degree of protection offered to the consumer. Where these are appropriate, they shall be product-type specific and only applied at the point of the food chain as specified in the regulation.

In situations of non-compliance with microbiological criteria, depending on the assessment of the risk to the consumer, the point in the food chain and the product-type specified, the regulatory control actions may be sorting, reprocessing, rejection or destruction of product, and/or further investigation to determine appropriate actions to be taken.

3.1.2   Application by a food business operator
In addition to checking compliance with regulatory provisions (see Section 3.1.1), microbiological criteria may be applied by food business operators to formulate design requirements and to examine end products as one of the measures to verify and/or validate the efficacy of the HACCP plan.

Such criteria will be specific for the product and the stage in the food chain at which they will apply. They may be stricter than the criteria used for regulatory purposes and should, as such, not be used for legal action.

3.2   Microbiological criteria are not normally suitable for monitoring critical limits as defined in "Hazard Analysis and Critical Control Point (HACCP) system and guidelines for its application" (Annex to CAC/RCP 1-1969). Monitoring procedures must be able to detect loss of control at a Critical Control Point (CCP). Monitoring should provide this information in time for corrective actions to be taken to regain control before there is a need to reject the product. Consequently, online measurements of physical and chemical parameters are often preferred to microbiological testing because results are often available more rapidly and at the production site. Moreover, the establishment of critical limits may need other considerations than those described in this document.

4.   GENERAL CONSIDERATIONS CONCERNING PRINCIPLES FOR ESTABLISHING AND APPLYING MICROBIOLOGICAL CRITERIA

4.1   A microbiological criterion should be established and applied only where there is a definite need and where its application is practical. Such need is demonstrated, for example, by epidemiological evidence that the food under consideration may represent a public health risk and that a criterion is meaningful for consumer protection, or as the result of a risk assessment. The criterion should be technically attainable by applying good manufacturing practices (Codes of practice).

4.2   To fulfil the purposes of a microbiological criterion, consideration should be given to:
- the evidence of actual or potential hazards to health;
- the microbiological status of the raw material(s);
- the effect of processing on the microbiological status of the food;
- the likelihood and consequences of microbial contamination and/or growth during subsequent handling, storage and use;
- the category(s) of consumers concerned;
- the cost/benefit ratio associated with the application of the criterion; and
- the intended use of the food.

4.3   The number and size of analytical units per lot tested should be as stated in the sampling plan and should not be modified. However, a lot should not be subjected to repeated testing in order to bring the lot into compliance.

5. MICROBIOLOGICAL ASPECTS OF CRITERIA

5.1 Micro-organisms, parasites and their toxins/metabolites of importance in a particular food

5.1.1 For the purpose of this document, these include:
- bacteria, viruses, yeasts, moulds and algae;
- parasitic protozoa and helminths;
- their toxins/metabolites.

5.1.2 The micro-organisms included in a criterion should be widely accepted as relevant – as pathogens, as indicator organisms or as spoilage organisms – to the particular food and technology. Organisms whose significance in the specified food is doubtful should not be included in a criterion.

5.1.3 The mere finding, with a presence–absence test, of certain organisms known to cause foodborne illness (e.g. *Clostridium perfringens, Staphylococcus aureus* and *Vibrio parahaemolyticus*) does not necessarily indicate a threat to public health.

5.1.4 Where pathogens can be detected directly and reliably, consideration should be given to testing for them in preference to testing for indicator organisms. If a test for an indicator organism is applied, there should be a clear statement whether the test is used to indicate unsatisfactory hygienic practices or a health hazard.

5.2 Microbiological methods

5.2.1 Whenever possible, only methods for which the reliability (accuracy, reproducibility, inter- and intra-laboratory variation) has been statistically established in comparative or collaborative studies in several laboratories should be used. Moreover, preference should be given to methods that have been validated for the commodity concerned preferably in relation to reference methods elaborated by international organizations. While methods should be the most sensitive and reproducible for the purpose, methods to be used for in-plant testing might often sacrifice to some degree sensitivity and reproducibility in the interest of speed and simplicity. They should, however, have been proved to give a sufficiently reliable estimate of the information needed.

Methods used to determine the suitability for consumption of highly perishable foods, or foods with a short shelf-life, should be chosen wherever possible so that the results of microbiological examinations are available before the foods are consumed or exceed their shelf-life.

5.2.2 The microbiological methods specified should be reasonable with regard to complexity, availability of media, equipment, etc., and ease of interpretation, time required and costs.

5.3   Microbiological limits

5.3.1   Limits used in criteria should be based on microbiological data appropriate to the food and should be applicable to a variety of similar products. They should therefore be based on data gathered at various production establishments operating under good hygienic practices and applying the HACCP system.

In the establishment of microbiological limits, any changes in the microflora likely to occur during storage and distribution (e.g. decrease or increase in numbers) should be taken into account.

5.3.2   Microbiological limits should take into consideration the risk associated with the micro-organisms and the conditions under which the food is expected to be handled and consumed. Microbiological limits should also take account of the likelihood of uneven distribution of micro-organisms in the food and the inherent variability of the analytical procedure.

5.3.3   If a criterion requires the absence of a particular micro-organism, the size and number of the analytical unit (as well as the number of analytical sample units) should be indicated.

6.   SAMPLING PLANS, METHODS AND HANDLING

6.1   A sampling plan includes the sampling procedure and the decision criteria to be applied to a lot, based on examination of a prescribed number of sample units and subsequent analytical units of a stated size by defined methods. A well-designed sampling plan defines the probability of detecting micro-organisms in a lot, but it should be borne in mind that no sampling plan can ensure the absence of a particular organism. Sampling plans should be administratively and economically feasible.

In particular, the choice of sampling plans should take into account:
- risks to public health associated with the hazard;
- the susceptibility of the target group of consumers;
- the heterogeneity of distribution of micro-organisms where variables sampling plans are employed; and
- the acceptable quality level[1] and the desired statistical probability of accepting a non-conforming lot.

For many applications, 2-or 3-class attribute plans may prove useful.[2]

---

[1] The acceptable quality level (AQL) is the percentage of non-conforming sample units in the entire lot for which the sampling plan will indicate lot acceptance for a prescribed probability (usually 95 percent).

[2] See International Commission on Microbiological Specification for Foods. 1986 *Microorganisms in foods, 2. Sampling for microbiological analysis. Principles and specific applications*. 2nd Edition. Oxford, UK, Blackwell Scientific Publications.

6.2   The statistical performance characteristics or operating characteristics curve should be provided in the sampling plan. Performance characteristics provide specific information to estimate the probability of accepting a non-conforming lot. The sampling method should be defined in the sampling plan. The time between taking the field samples and analysis should be as short as reasonably possible, and during transport to the laboratory the conditions (e.g. temperature) should not allow increase or decrease of the numbers of the target organism, so that the results reflect – within the limitations given by the sampling plan – the microbiological conditions of the lot.

7. REPORTING

7.1   The test report should give the information needed for complete identification of the sample, the sampling plan, the test method, the results and, where appropriate, their interpretation.

PRINCIPLES AND GUIDELINES FOR THE CONDUCT OF MICROBIOLOGICAL RISK ASSESSMENT

CAC/GL 30-1999

PRINCIPLES AND GUIDELINES FOR THE CONDUCT OF MICROBIOLOGICAL RISK ASSESSMENT

CAC/GL 30-1999

INTRODUCTION

Risks from microbiological hazards are of immediate and serious concern to human health. Microbiological risk analysis is a process consisting of three components: risk assessment, risk management, and risk communication. Its overall objective is to ensure public health protection. This document deals with risk assessment, which is a key element in ensuring that sound science is used to establish standards, guidelines and other recommendations for food safety to enhance consumer protection and facilitate international trade. The microbiological risk assessment process should include quantitative information to the greatest extent possible in the estimation of risk. A microbiological risk assessment should be conducted using a structured approach such as that described in this document. This document will be of primary interest to governments although other organizations, companies and other interested parties that need to prepare a microbiological risk assessment will find it valuable. As microbiological risk assessment is a developing science, implementation of these Guidelines may require a period of time and may also require specialized training in the countries that consider it necessary. This may be particularly the case for developing countries. Although microbiological risk assessment is the primary focus of this document, the method can also be applied to certain other classes of biological hazards.

1. SCOPE

The scope of this document applies to risk assessment of microbiological hazards in food.

2. DEFINITIONS

The definitions cited here are to facilitate the understanding of certain words or phrases used in this document.

Where available, the definitions are those adopted for microbiological, chemical or physical agents and risk management and risk communication on an interim basis at the 22nd Session of the Codex Alimentarius Commission. The Codex Alimentarius Commission adopted these definitions on an interim basis because they are subject to modification in the light of developments in the science of risk analysis and as a result of efforts to harmonize similar definitions across various disciplines.

Dose-response assessment The determination of the relationship between the magnitude of exposure (dose) to a chemical, biological or physical agent and the severity and/or frequency of associated adverse health effects (response).

Exposure assessment The qualitative and/or quantitative evaluation of the likely intake of biological, chemical and physical agents via food as well as exposures from other sources if relevant.

Hazard A biological, chemical or physical agent in, or condition of, food with the potential to cause an adverse health effect.

Hazard characterization The qualitative and/or quantitative evaluation of the nature of the adverse health effects associated with the hazard. For the purpose of microbiological risk assessment, the concerns relate to micro-organisms and/or their toxins.

Hazard identification The identification of biological, chemical and physical agents capable of causing adverse health effects and which may be present in a particular food or group of foods.

Quantitative risk assessment A risk assessment that provides numerical expressions of risk and indication of the attendant uncertainties (stated in the 1995 Expert Consultation definition of risk analysis).

Qualitative risk assessment A risk assessment based on data that, while forming an inadequate basis for numerical risk estimations, nonetheless, when conditioned by prior expert knowledge and identification of attendant uncertainties, permit risk ranking or separation into descriptive categories of risk.

Risk A function of the probability of an adverse health effect and the severity of that effect, consequential to a hazard(s) in food.

Risk analysis A process consisting of three components: risk assessment, risk management and risk communication.

Risk assessment A scientifically based process consisting of the following steps: (i) hazard identification, (ii) hazard characterization, (iii) exposure assessment, and (iv) risk characterization.

Risk characterization The process of determining the qualitative and/or quantitative estimation, including attendant uncertainties, of the probability of occurrence and severity of known or potential adverse health effects in a given population based on hazard identification, hazard characterization and exposure assessment.

Risk communication The interactive exchange of information and opinions concerning risk and risk management among risk assessors, risk managers, consumers and other interested parties.

Risk estimate Output of risk characterization.

Risk management The process of weighing policy alternatives in the light of the results of risk assessment and, if required, selecting and implementing appropriate control[1] options, including regulatory measures.

Sensitivity analysis A method used to examine the behaviour of a model by measuring the variation in its outputs resulting from changes to its inputs.

Transparent Characteristics of a process where the rationale, the logic of development, constraints, assumptions, value judgements, decisions, limitations and uncertainties

---

[1] Control means prevention, elimination or reduction of hazards and/or minimization of risks.

of the expressed determination are fully and systematically stated, documented and accessible for review.

Uncertainty analysis A method used to estimate the uncertainty associated with model inputs, assumptions and structure/form.

3.   GENERAL PRINCIPLES OF MICROBIOLOGICAL RISK ASSESSMENT

1.   Microbiological risk assessment should be soundly based upon science.
2.   There should be a functional separation between risk assessment and risk management.
3.   Microbiological risk assessment should be conducted according to a structured approach that includes hazard identification, hazard characterization, exposure assessment and risk characterization.
4.   A microbiological risk assessment should clearly state the purpose of the exercise, including the form of risk estimate that will be the output.
5.   The conduct of a microbiological risk assessment should be transparent.
6.   Any constraints that affect the risk assessment, such as cost, resources or time, should be identified and their possible consequences described.
7.   The risk estimate should contain a description of uncertainty and where the uncertainty arose during the risk assessment process.
8.   Data should be such that uncertainty in the risk estimate can be determined; data and data collection systems should, as far as possible, be of sufficient quality and precision that uncertainty in the risk estimate is minimized.
9.   A microbiological risk assessment should explicitly consider the dynamics of microbiological growth, survival and death in foods and the complexity of the interaction (including sequelae) between human and agent following consumption as well as the potential for further spread.
10.   Wherever possible, risk estimates should be reassessed over time by comparison with independent human illness data.
11.   A microbiological risk assessment may need re-evaluation, as new relevant information becomes available.

4.   GUIDELINES FOR APPLICATION

These Guidelines provide an outline of the elements of a microbiological risk assessment indicating the types of decisions that need to be considered at each step.

4.1   General considerations

The elements of risk analysis are: risk assessment, risk management, and risk communication. The functional separation of risk assessment from risk management helps ensure that the risk assessment process is unbiased. However, certain interactions are needed for a comprehensive and systematic risk assessment process. These may include ranking of hazards and risk assessment policy decisions. Where risk management issues are taken into account in risk assessment, the decision-making process should be transparent. It is the transparent unbiased nature of the process that is important, not who the assessor is or who the manager is.

Whenever practical, efforts should be made to provide a risk assessment process that allows contributions by interested parties. Contributions by interested parties in the risk assessment process can improve the transparency of the risk assessment, increase the quality of risk assessments through additional expertise and information, and facilitate risk communication by increasing the credibility and acceptance of the results of the risk assessment.

Scientific evidence may be limited, incomplete or conflicting. In such cases, transparent informed decisions will have to be made on how to complete the risk assessment process. The importance of using high-quality information when conducting a risk assessment is to reduce uncertainty and to increase the reliability of the risk estimate. The use of quantitative information is encouraged to the extent possible, but the value and utility of qualitative information should not be discounted.

It should be recognized that sufficient resources will not always be available and constraints are likely to be imposed on the risk assessment that will influence the quality of the risk estimate. Where such resource constraints apply, it is important for transparency purposes that these constraints be described in the formal record. Where appropriate, the record should include an evaluation of the impact of the resource constraints on the risk assessment.

4.2 Statement of purpose of risk assessment

At the beginning of the work, the specific purpose of the particular risk assessment being carried out should be clearly stated. The output form and possible output alternatives of the risk assessment should be defined. Output might, for example, take the form of an estimate of the prevalence of illness, or an estimate of annual rate (incidence of human illness per 100 000) or an estimate of the rate of human illness and severity per eating occurrence.

The microbiological risk assessment may require a preliminary investigation phase. In this phase, evidence to support farm-to-table modelling of risk might be structured or mapped into the framework of risk assessment.

4.3 Hazard identification

For microbial agents, the purpose of hazard identification is to identify the micro-organisms or the microbial toxins of concern with food. Hazard identification will predominately be a qualitative process. Hazards can be identified from relevant data sources. Information on hazards can be obtained from scientific literature, from databases such as those in the food industry, government agencies and relevant international organizations and through solicitation of opinions of experts. Relevant information includes data in areas such as: clinical studies, epidemiological studies and surveillance, laboratory animal studies, investigations of the characteristics of micro-organisms, the interaction between micro-organisms and their environment through the food chain from primary production up to and including consumption, and studies on analogous micro-organisms and situations.

4.4 Exposure assessment

Exposure assessment includes an assessment of the extent of actual or anticipated human exposure. For microbiological agents, exposure assessments might be based on the potential extent of food contamination by a particular agent or its toxins, and on dietary information. Exposure assessment should specify the unit of food that is of interest, i.e. the portion size in most/all cases of acute illness.

Factors that must be considered for exposure assessment include the frequency of contamination of foods by the pathogenic agent and its level in those foods over time. For example, these factors are influenced by: the characteristics of the pathogenic agent; the microbiological ecology of the food; the initial contamination of the raw material, including considerations of regional differences and seasonality of production; the level of sanitation and process controls; the methods of processing, packaging, distribution and storage of the foods; as well as any preparation steps such as cooking and holding. Another factor that must be considered in the assessment is patterns of consumption. This relates to socio-economic and cultural backgrounds, ethnicity, seasonality, age differences (population demographics), regional differences, and consumer preferences and behaviour. Other factors to be considered include: the role of the food handler as a source of contamination, the amount of hand contact with the product, and the potential impact of abusive environmental time/temperature relationships.

Microbial pathogen levels can be dynamic and while they may be kept low, for example, by proper time/temperature controls during food processing, they can substantially increase with abuse conditions (for example, improper food storage temperatures or cross-contamination from other foods). Therefore, the exposure assessment should describe the pathway from production to consumption. Scenarios can be constructed to predict the range of possible exposures. The scenarios might reflect effects of processing, such as hygienic design, cleaning and disinfection, as well as the time/temperature and other conditions of the food history, food handling and consumption patterns, regulatory controls and surveillance systems.

Exposure assessment estimates the level, within various levels of uncertainty, of microbiological pathogens or microbiological toxins, and the likelihood of their occurrence in foods at the time of consumption. Qualitatively, foods can be categorized according to: the likelihood that the foodstuff will or will not be contaminated at its source; whether or not the food can support the growth of the pathogen of concern; whether there is substantial potential for abusive handling of the food; or whether the food will be subjected to a heat process. The presence, growth, survival or death of micro-organisms, including pathogens in foods, are influenced by processing and packaging, the storage environment, including the temperature of storage, the relative humidity of the environment, and the gaseous composition of the atmosphere. Other relevant factors include pH, moisture content or water activity (A_w), nutrient content, the presence of antimicrobial substances, and competing microflora. Predictive microbiology can be a useful tool in an exposure assessment.

4.5   **Hazard characterization**
This step provides a qualitative or quantitative description of the severity and duration of adverse effects that may result from the ingestion of a micro-organism or its toxin in food. A dose-response assessment should be performed if the data are obtainable.

There are several important factors that need to be considered in hazard characterization. These are related to both the micro-organism and the human host. In relation to the micro-organism, the following are important: micro-organisms are capable of replicating; the virulence and infectivity of micro-organisms can change depending on their interaction with the host and the environment; genetic material can be transferred between micro-organisms leading to the transfer of characteristics such as antibiotic resistance and virulence factors; micro-organisms can be spread through secondary and tertiary transmission; the onset of clinical symptoms can be substantially delayed following exposure; micro-organisms can persist in certain individuals leading to continued excretion of the micro-organism and continued risk of spread of infection; low doses of some micro-organisms can in some cases cause a severe effect; and the attributes of a food may alter the microbial pathogenicity, e.g. high fat content of a food vehicle.

In relation to the host, the following may be important: genetic factors such as human leucocyte antigen (HLA) type; increased susceptibility due to breakdowns of physiological barriers; individual host susceptibility characteristics such as age, pregnancy, nutrition, health and medication status, concurrent infections, immune status and previous exposure history; population characteristics such as population immunity, access to and use of medical care, and persistence of the organism in the population.

A desirable feature of hazard characterization is ideally establishing a dose-response relationship. When establishing a dose-response relationship, the different end-points, such as infection or illness, should be taken into consideration. In the absence of a known dose-response relationship, risk assessment tools such as expert elicitations could be used to consider various factors, such as infectivity, necessary to describe hazard characterizations. Additionally, experts may be able to devise ranking systems so that they can be used to characterize severity and/or duration of disease.

4.6   **Risk characterization**
Risk characterization represents the integration of the hazard identification, hazard characterization and exposure assessment determinations to obtain a risk estimate; providing a qualitative or quantitative estimate of the likelihood and severity of the adverse effects which could occur in a given population, including a description of the uncertainties associated with these estimates. These estimates can be assessed by comparison with independent epidemiological data that relate hazards to disease prevalence.

Risk characterization brings together all of the qualitative or quantitative information of the previous steps to provide a soundly based estimate of risk for a given population.

Risk characterization depends on available data and expert judgements. The weight of evidence integrating quantitative and qualitative data may permit only a qualitative estimate of risk.

The degree of confidence in the final estimation of risk will depend on the variability, uncertainty and assumptions identified in all previous steps. Differentiation of uncertainty and variability is important in subsequent selections of risk management options. Uncertainty is associated with the data themselves, and with the choice of model. Data uncertainties include those that might arise in the evaluation and extrapolation of information obtained from epidemiological, microbiological and laboratory animal studies. Uncertainties arise whenever attempts are made to use data concerning the occurrence of certain phenomena obtained under one set of conditions to make estimations or predictions about phenomena likely to occur under other sets of conditions for which data are not available. Biological variation includes the differences in virulence that exist in microbiological populations and variability in susceptibility within the human population and particular subpopulations.

It is important to demonstrate the influence of the estimates and assumptions used in risk assessment; for quantitative risk assessment, this can be done using sensitivity and uncertainty analyses.

4.7   Documentation

The risk assessment should be fully and systematically documented and communicated to the risk manager. Understanding any limitations that influenced a risk assessment is essential for transparency of the process that is important in decision-making. For example, expert judgements should be identified and their rationale explained. To ensure a transparent risk assessment, a formal record, including a summary, should be prepared and made available to interested independent parties so that other risk assessors can repeat and critique the work. The formal record and summary should indicate any constraints, uncertainties and assumptions and their impact on the risk assessment.

4.8   Reassessment

Surveillance programmes can provide an ongoing opportunity to reassess the public health risks associated with pathogens in foods as new relevant information and data become available. Microbiological risk assessors may have the opportunity to compare the predicted risk estimate from microbiological risk assessment models with reported human illness data for the purpose of gauging the reliability of the predicted estimate. This comparison emphasizes the iterative nature of modelling. When new data become available, a microbiological risk assessment may need to be revisited.

PRINCIPLES AND GUIDELINES FOR THE CONDUCT OF MICROBIOLOGICAL RISK MANAGEMENT (MRM)

CAC/GL 63-2007

Adopted in 2007. Annex 2 on "Guidance on microbiological risk management metrics" adopted in 2008.

PRINCIPLES AND GUIDELINES FOR THE CONDUCT OF MICROBIOLOGICAL RISK MANAGEMENT (MRM)

CAC/GL 63-2007

INTRODUCTION

Diseases caused by foodborne microbial hazards[1] constitute a worldwide public health concern. During the past several decades, the incidence of foodborne diseases has increased in many parts of the world. Foodborne threats occur for a number of reasons. These include microbial adaptation, changes in food production systems, including new feeding practices, changes in animal husbandry, agronomic processes, and food technology, increase in international trade, susceptible populations and travel, changes in lifestyle and consumer demand, and changes in human demographics and behaviour. The globalization of food markets has increased the challenge to manage these risks.

Effective management of risks arising from microbial hazards is technically complex. Food safety has been traditionally, and will continue to be, the responsibility of industry operating an array of control measures relating to the food hygiene within an overall regulatory framework. Recently, risk analysis, involving its component parts of risk assessment, risk management and risk communication, has been introduced as a new approach in evaluating and controlling microbial hazards to help protect the health of consumers and ensure fair practices in food trade. It could also facilitate the judgement of equivalence of food safety control systems.

This document should be read in close conjunction with the "Working Principles for risk analysis for application in the framework of the Codex Alimentarius"[2] and the *Principles and Guidelines for the conduct of microbiological risk assessment* (CAC/GL 30–1999). Countries, organizations and individuals involved with microbiological risk management (MRM) are encouraged to utilize these Guidelines in concert with technical information developed by the World Health Organization, the Food and Agriculture Organization of the United Nations and the Codex Alimentarius (e.g. *FAO/WHO Expert Consultation on risk management and food safety*, Food and Nutrition Paper No. 65, Rome 1997; *WHO Expert Consultation – the interaction between assessors and managers of microbiological hazards in food*, Kiel, Germany, March 2000; *Principles and guidelines for incorporating microbiological risk assessment in the development of food safety standards, guidelines and related texts*, Report of a Joint FAO/WHO Consultation, Kiel, Germany, March 2002; *The use of microbiological risk assessment outputs to develop practical risk management strategies: metrics to improve food safety,* Report of a Joint FAO/WHO Expert Meeting, Kiel, Germany, April 2006).

---

[1] Foodborne microbial hazards include (but are not limited to) pathogenic bacteria, viruses, algae, protozoa, fungi, parasites, prions, toxins and other harmful metabolites of microbial origin.

[2] See Codex Alimentarius Commission, *Procedural Manual.*

1. SCOPE

These Principles and Guidelines provide a framework for the MRM process and are intended for use by Codex and countries,[3] as appropriate. They also provide guidance on the application of microbiological risk assessment (MRA) within the MRM process. Where specific recommendations apply only to Codex, or only to countries, this is so noted in the text. This document also provides useful guidance for other interested parties in implementing risk management options, such as industry[4] and consumers who are involved in MRM on a day-to-day basis.

2. DEFINITIONS

The definitions of risk analysis terms related to food safety incorporated in the *Procedural Manual* of the Codex Alimentarius Commission,[5] shall apply. See definitions **of hazard, risk, risk analysis, risk assessment, hazard identification, hazard characterization, dose-response assessment, exposure assessment, risk characterization, risk management, risk communication, risk assessment policy, risk profile, risk estimate, food safety objective (FSO), performance objective (PO), performance criterion (PC), traceability/product tracing** and **equivalence**.

The definitions from the "Hazard Analysis and Critical Control Point (HACCP) system and guidelines for its application",[6] e.g. **control measure, step** or **critical control point**; the definition of a **microbiological criterion** included in the *Principles for the application of microbiological criteria for food* (CAC/GL 21-1997); and the definition of **interested parties** included in the "Working Principles for risk analysis for application in the framework of the Codex Alimentarius"[7] shall apply too.

The definition of the appropriate level of protection (**ALOP**) is the one in the World Trade Organization (WTO) Agreement on the application of sanitary and phytosanitary measures (SPS Agreement).

The definitions of **validation, verification** and **food safety control system** are under development in the draft *Guidelines for the validation of food safety control measures*.

---

[3] For the purpose of this document, each time the terms "country", "government", "national" are used, the provision applies both to Codex Members (Rule I) and Codex Member Organizations (Rule II), i.e. Regional Economic Integration Organizations (REIOs) – see Codex Alimentarius Commission, *Procedural Manual*.

[4] For the purpose of this document, it is understood that industry includes all relevant sectors associated with the production, storage and handling of food, from primary production through retail and food service level (adapted from "Working Principles for risk analysis for application in the framework of the Codex Alimentarius").

[5] Codex Alimentarius Commission, *Procedural Manual*.

[6] Annex to *Recommended International Code of Practice – General Principles of food hygiene* (CAC/RCP 1-1969).

[7] Codex Alimentarius Commission, *Procedural Manual*.

Risk manager[8] is defined as follows: a national or international governmental organization with responsibility for MRM.

3. GENERAL PRINCIPLES FOR MRM

- PRINCIPLE 1: Protection of human health is the primary objective in MRM.
- PRINCIPLE 2: MRM should take into account the whole food chain.
- PRINCIPLE 3: MRM should follow a structured approach.
- PRINCIPLE 4: MRM process should be transparent, consistent and fully documented.
- PRINCIPLE 5: Risk managers should ensure effective consultations with relevant interested parties.
- PRINCIPLE 6: Risk managers should ensure effective interaction with risk assessors.
- PRINCIPLE 7: Risk managers should take account of risks resulting from regional differences in hazards in the food chain and regional differences in available risk management options.
- PRINCIPLE 8: MRM decisions should be subject to monitoring and review and, if necessary, revision.

4. GENERAL CONSIDERATIONS

Codex and government decisions and recommendations have as their primary objective the protection of the health of consumers. Decision-making should be timely to achieve that objective. In the MRM process, the ALOP is a key concept, as it is a reflection of a particular country's expressed public health goals for foodborne risks.

MRM should address the food chains as individual continuums when considering means for controlling the public health risks associated with food. This should typically include primary production (including feeds, agricultural practices, and environmental conditions leading to the contamination of crops and animals), product design and processing, transport, storage, distribution, marketing, preparation and consumption. This should include both domestic and imported products to the extent feasible.

MRM should follow a structured approach that includes preliminary MRM activities, identification and selection of MRM options, implementation of MRM activities, and monitoring and review of the options taken.

In order to facilitate a broader understanding by interested parties, the MRM process should be transparent and fully documented. Risk managers should articulate and implement uniform procedures and practices to be used in the development and

---

[8] The definition of risk manager is derived from the definition for risk management, which does not include all of the individuals who are involved in the implementation phase and related activities associated with MRM, i.e. MRM decisions are largely implemented by industry and other interested parties. The focus of the definition on risk manager is restricted to governmental organizations with authority to decide on the acceptability of risk levels associated to foodborne hazards.

implementation of MRM, the determination of MRA policy, the establishment of MRM priorities, the allocation of resources (e.g. human, financial, time) and the determination of the factors[9] to be used in the evaluation of MRM options. They should ensure that the options selected protect the health of consumers, are scientifically justifiable, are proportionate to the risk identified and are not more restrictive of trade or technological innovation than required to achieve the ALOP. Risk managers should ensure that decisions are practicable and effective, and, where appropriate, enforceable.

Risk managers should ensure effective and timely consultation with all relevant interested parties and provide a sound basis for understanding the MRM decision, its rationale and implications. The extent and nature of public consultation will depend on the urgency, complexity and uncertainties related to the risk and the management strategies being considered. Decisions and recommendations on MRM should be documented and, where appropriate, clearly identified in Codex or national standards and regulations so as to facilitate a wider understanding of the conduct of MRM.

The mandate given by risk managers to risk assessors relating to the conduct of an MRA should be as clear as possible. Interaction should allow risk managers to be informed by risk assessors of any constraints, data gaps, uncertainties, assumptions and their impact on the MRA. Where there is disagreement among the risk assessors, the risk managers should be informed of the minority opinions and these differences should be documented.

MRM decisions regarding foodborne hazards will vary according to the regional microbial conditions. MRM should take into account the diversity of production methods and processes, inspection, monitoring and verification systems, sampling and testing methods, distribution and marketing systems, consumer food-use patterns, consumers' perceptions and the prevalence of specific adverse health effects.

MRM should be an iterative process and decisions made should be subject to timely review, taking into account all relevant newly generated data, with a goal of further risk reduction and public health improvement.

5. PRELIMINARY MICROBIOLOGICAL RISK MANAGEMENT ACTIVITIES

5.1   Identification of a microbiological food safety issue
A food safety issue arises where one or more foodborne microbial hazard(s) is/are known or thought to be associated with one or many food(s) and thus require(s) consideration of a risk manager. The risk manager follows the MRM process to evaluate and, where necessary, manage the associated risk. At the start of this process, the food safety issue should be clearly identified and communicated from the risk managers to risk assessors, as well as affected consumers and industry.

---

[9]   See Codex Alimentarius Commission, *Procedural Manual*.

Food safety issue identification may be performed by the risk manager or be the result of collaboration between different interested parties. Within Codex, a food safety issue may be raised by a member government, or by an intergovernmental or observer organization.

Food safety issues may be identified on the basis of information arising from a variety of sources, such as surveys of the prevalence and concentration of hazards in the food chain or the environment, human disease surveillance data, epidemiological or clinical studies, laboratory studies, scientific, technological or medical advances, lack of compliance with standards, recommendations of experts, public input, etc.

Some food safety issues may require that an immediate action[10] be taken by the risk manager without further scientific consideration (e.g. requiring withdrawal/recall of contaminated products). Countries will often not be able to delay taking an immediate action when there is an imminent public health concern demanding an urgent response. Such measures should be temporary, clearly communicated as well as subject to review within a time frame.

When there is evidence that a risk to human health exists but scientific data are insufficient or incomplete, it may be appropriate for countries to select a provisional decision, while obtaining additional information that may inform and, if necessary, modify the provisional decision. In those instances, the provisional nature of the decision should be communicated to all interested parties and the time frame or circumstances under which the provisional decision will be reconsidered (e.g. reconsideration after the completion of an MRA) should be articulated when the decision is communicated initially.

5.2 Microbiological risk profile

The risk profile is a description of a food safety problem and its context that presents, in a concise form, the current state of knowledge related to a food safety issue, describes potential MRM options that have been identified to date, when any, and the food safety policy context that will influence further possible actions. Annex I provides information about suggested risk profile elements for guidance to risk managers at the national level, and for bringing forward newly proposed work within the Codex Committee on Food Hygiene.

Consideration of the information given in the risk profile may result in a range of initial decisions, such as commissioning an MRA, gathering more information or developing risk knowledge at the level of the risk manager, implementing an immediate and/or temporary decision (see Section 5.1 above). National governments may also base their MRM decisions on Codex standards, recommendations and guidance where available.

---

[10] The International Health Regulation (2005) agreement gives provisions for appropriate measures in case of public health emergencies. The *Principles and Guidelines for the exchange of information in food safety emergency situation* (CAC/GL 19-1995) defines a food safety emergency as a situation whether accidental or intentional that is identified by a competent authority as constituting a serious and as yet uncontrolled foodborne risk to public health that requires urgent action. Emergency measures may be part of immediate action.

In some cases, the risk profile could give enough information for identification and selection of MRM options. In other cases, no further action may be needed.

The risk profile provides an initial analysis that describes possible MRM options. The MRM options can take the form of a draft MRM guidance document that will be introduced into the Codex step process (e.g. codes of practice, guidance documents, microbiological specifications).

5.3 Risk assessment policy

Refer to the "Working Principles for risk analysis for the application in the framework of the Codex Alimentarius".[11] National governments should establish an MRA policy relevant to their circumstances, in advance of the microbiological risk assessment.

Risk assessment policy-setting is a risk management responsibility, which should be carried out in full collaboration with risk assessors. Establishing a risk assessment policy protects the scientific integrity of the risk assessment and offers guidance to balance value judgements, policy choices, adverse health parameters for presenting risk to human health, source of data to be considered, and management of data gaps and uncertainties during the course of the assessment. The risk assessment policy could be of a generic nature or MRA-specific, and should be documented to ensure consistency, clarity and transparency.

5.4 Microbiological risk assessment

Risk managers may commission an MRA to provide an objective, systematic evaluation of relevant scientific knowledge to help make an informed decision.

The risk manager should refer to the *Principles and Guidelines for the conduct of microbiological risk assessment* (CAC/GL 30-1999). It is important to ensure that a clear mandate is given to risk assessors and that the MRA meets the needs of the risk manager. It is also important that the MRA be adequately reviewed by the scientific community and, where appropriate, the public.

The outputs of the MRA should be presented by risk assessors in such a manner that they can be properly understood and utilized by risk managers in the evaluation of the suitability of different MRM options to manage the food safety issue. Generally, the presentation is conveyed in two different formats: a fully detailed technical report and an interpretative summary for a broader audience.

For the best use of an MRA, risk managers should be fully informed of the strengths and limitations (key assumptions, key data gaps, uncertainty and variability in the data, and their influences on the outcomes), including a pragmatic appreciation of uncertainties associated to the MRA study and its outputs. Risk managers, in consultation with risk assessors, should then decide whether the MRA is in developing and/or evaluating and deciding on suitable MRM activities, or deciding on provisional MRM options.

---

[11] See Codex Alimentarius Commission, *Procedural Manual*.

6. IDENTIFICATION AND SELECTION OF MRM OPTIONS

6.1   Identification of the available MRM options for Codex and countries

The risk manager needs to ensure that MRM options are identified and the acceptable one(s) selected for subsequent implementation by relevant interested parties. In this, risk managers need to consider the suitability of MRM options to reduce the risk posed by a food safety issue to an appropriate level and any practical issues regarding the implementation of the selected MRM options that need to be managed.

Examples of potential MRM options (used either alone or in combination) available for Codex or countries, as appropriate, are listed below.

6.1.1   Codex

- Elaboration of standards and related texts.[12]

6.1.2   Countries

- Establish regulatory requirements.
- Develop (or encourage the development of) specific documents and guides e.g. good agricultural practices (GAPs), good manufacturing practices (GMPs), good hygienic practices (GHPs), Hazard Analysis and Critical Control Point (HACCP).
- Adopt or adapt Codex Standards and related texts to the national situation.
- Define an FSO for a particular food safety issue, leaving flexibility to industry to select appropriate control measures to meet it.
- Establish control measures specifying relevant requirements for industries that do not have the means to establish appropriate measures themselves or who adopt such control measures, including as appropriate metrics[13] at specific stages of the food/feed[14] chain where they are of critical importance to the performance of the overall chain.
- Establish requirements for inspection and audit procedures, certification or approval procedures.
- Require import certificates for certain products.
- Promulgate awareness and develop educational and training programmes to communicate that:
  - prevention of contamination and/or introduction of hazards should be addressed at all relevant stages in the food/feed chain;
  - rapid withdrawal/recall of food/feed procedures are in place, including appropriate traceability/product tracing for effectiveness;

---

[12] When there is evidence that a risk to human health exists but scientific data are insufficient or incomplete, the Codex Alimentarius Commission should not proceed to elaborate a standard but should consider elaborating a related text, such as a code of practice, provided that such a text would be supported by the available scientific evidence, "Working Principles for risk analysis for application in the framework of the Codex Alimentarius", Codex Alimentarius Commission, *Procedural Manual.*

[13] See *Principles and guidelines for incorporating microbiological risk assessment in the development of food safety standards, guidelines and related texts*, Report of a Joint FAO/WHO Consultation, Kiel, Germany, March 2002.

[14] In those instances where the presence of hazards in feed may affect the safety of foods derived from an animal, the microbiological profile of feed should be considered.

 – proper labelling includes information that instructs the consumer regarding safe handling practices and, where appropriate, briefly informs the consumer of the food safety issue.

6.2 Selection of MRM options

The selection of MRM options should be based on their ability to mitigate the risks effectively and on the practical feasibility and consequences of the options. Where available, an MRA can often help in the evaluation and selection of MRM options.

The selection of MRM options that are both effective and feasible should generally include consideration of the following:
- planned control of hazards (e.g. with HACCP) is more effective than detecting and correcting food safety control system failures (e.g. lot-release microbiological testing of finished products);
- the population may be exposed to multiple potential sources of a particular hazard;
- the suitability of the option to be monitored, reviewed and revised during subsequent implementation;
- the capacity of the food businesses to manage food safety (e.g. human resources, size, type of operation). For instance, a more traditional approach may be selected for small and less-developed food businesses, rather than an FSO-driven approach.

6.2.1 Responsibility for selecting MRM options

The primary responsibility for selecting appropriate MRM options lies with the risk manager.

Risk assessors and other interested parties play an important role in this process by providing information that permits the evaluation and, if appropriate, comparison of different MRM options.

Whenever feasible, both Codex and countries should attempt to specify the level of control or risk reduction that is necessary (i.e. establish the stringency required for food safety control systems), while providing, to the extent feasible, some flexibility in options that the industry can use to achieve the appropriate level of control.

6.2.2 MRM options based on risk

The increasing adoption of risk analysis is allowing more transparent approaches for relating ALOP to the required stringency of the food safety control system, and for the comparison of MRM options for their suitability and, possibly, equivalence. This has allowed the use of traditional MRM options as well as the development of new MRM tools, e.g. FSO, PO and PC and the enhancement of the scientific basis of existing MRM tools, e.g. microbiological criteria (MC).

7. IMPLEMENTATION OF MRM OPTIONS

Implementation involves giving effect to the selected MRM option(s) and verifying compliance, i.e. ensuring that the MRM option(s) is/are implemented as intended. Implementation may involve different interested parties, including competent authorities, industry and consumers. Codex does not implement MRM options.

7.1   International intergovernmental organizations

Developing countries may need specific assistance in developing and selecting implementation strategies as well as in the area of education. Such assistance should be provided by international intergovernmental organizations, e.g. FAO and WHO, and developed countries in the spirit of the SPS Agreement.

7.2   Countries

The implementation strategy will depend on the MRM option(s) selected and should be developed within a consultative process with interested parties. Implementation can occur at different points in the food/feed chain and may involve more than one segment of the industry and consumers.

Once an MRM option is selected, risk managers should develop an implementation plan that describes how the option will be implemented, by whom, and when. In some situations, a stepwise phase-in implementation strategy could be considered, e.g. different-sized establishments or different sectors, in part based on risk and/or capability. Guidance and support may need to be provided, in particular for small and less-developed businesses.

To ensure transparency, risk managers should communicate decisions on MRM options to all interested parties, including the rationale, and how those affected will be expected to implement. To the extent that imports will be affected, other governments should be informed of the decision(s) and rationale in order to ensure their own MRM strategies achieve equivalence.

If the MRM options selected are provisional, the rationale and the expected time frame for finalizing the decision should be communicated.

Governments should ensure an appropriate regulatory framework and infrastructure, including adequately trained personnel and inspection staff, in order to enforce regulations and verify compliance. Inspection and targeted sampling plans may be applied at different steps of the food chain. The competent authorities should ensure that industry applies the appropriate good practices and, within the application of the HACCP system, effectively monitors CCPs and implements corrective actions and verification steps.

Governments should define an evaluation process to assess whether the MRM options have been properly implemented. This process should allow for adjustment of the implementation plan or of the MRM options, if the options selected are not successful in achieving the required level of control over the hazard. This is intended to provide short-term evaluation to allow modification, particularly for provisional MRM options, versus longer-term monitoring and review, as discussed in Sections 8.1 and 8.2.

7.3 Industry

Industry is responsible for developing and applying food safety control systems to give effect to the decisions on MRM options. Depending on the nature of the MRM option, this may require activities such as:

- establishing metrics that will achieve or contribute to established FSOs or other regulatory requirements;
- the identification of PC and design and implementation of appropriate combinations of validated control measures;
- monitoring and verification of the food safety control system or relevant parts thereof (e.g. control measures, good practices);
- application, as appropriate, of sampling plans for microbiological analyses;
- development of plans for corrective actions, that may include withdrawal/recall procedures, traceability/product tracing, etc.;
- effective communication with suppliers, customers and/or consumers, as appropriate;
- training or instruction of staff and internal communication.

Industry associations may find it beneficial to develop and provide guidance documents, training programmes, technical bulletins and other information that assists industry to implement control measures.

7.4 Consumer

Consumers can enhance both their personal and the public's health by being responsible for, adhering to, being informed of and following food safety-related instructions. Multiple means of providing this information to consumers should be undertaken, such as public education programmes, appropriate labelling and public interest messages. Consumer organizations can play a significant role in communicating this information to consumers.

8. MONITORING AND REVIEW

8.1 Monitoring

An essential part of the MRM process is the ongoing gathering, analysing and interpreting of data related to the performance of food safety control systems, which, in this context, is referred to as monitoring. Monitoring is essential to establish a baseline for comparing the effectiveness of new MRM activities. It also may provide information that the manager may use to determine what steps may be taken to achieve further improvements in the extent or efficiency of risk mitigation and public health. Risk management programmes should strive for continual improvement in public health.

Monitoring activities related to measuring the state of public health are, in most cases, the responsibility of national governments. For instance, surveillance of human populations and the analysis of human health data on a national level are generally conducted by countries. International organizations such as WHO provide guidance for establishing and implementing public health monitoring programmes.

Monitoring activities regarding microbial hazards may be needed at multiple points along the entire food chain to identify food safety issues and to assess public health and food safety status and trends. Monitoring should provide information on all aspects of risks from specific hazards and foods relevant to MRM, and is key to the generation of data for the development of a risk profile or an MRA as well as for the review of MRM activities. Monitoring should also include evaluating the effectiveness of consumer communication strategies.

Monitoring activities can include the collection and analysis of data derived from:
- surveillance of clinical diseases in humans, as well as diseases in plants and animals that can affect humans;
- epidemiological investigations of outbreaks and other special studies;
- surveillance based on laboratory tests of pathogens isolated from humans, plants, animals, foods and food-processing environments for pertinent foodborne hazards;
- data on environmental hygiene practices and procedures;
- behavioural risk factor surveillance of food worker and consumer habits and practices.

When establishing or redesigning monitoring systems in countries, the following aspects should be considered:
- A public health surveillance system should be able to estimate the proportion of illnesses and death that is truly foodborne and the major food vehicles, processes and food-handling practices responsible for each hazard.
- Interdisciplinary teams of epidemiologists and food safety experts should be formed to investigate foodborne illness to identify the food vehicles and the series of events that lead to illnesses.
- Microbiological and/or physicochemical indicators of a particular intervention should be considered together with human disease data to evaluate programmatic impact on public health.
- Countries should work towards harmonization of surveillance definitions and reporting rules, protocols and data management systems to facilitate comparison between countries of incidence and trends of the illnesses and microbiological data in the food chain.

8.2 Review of MRM activities

The effectiveness and appropriateness of the MRM activities selected, and of the implementation thereof, need to be reviewed. Review is an integral part of the MRM process and ideally should take place at a predetermined moment in time or whenever relevant information becomes available. Criteria for review should be established as part of the implementation plan. Review may lead to a change in the MRM activities.

Planning periodic review of MRM activities is the best way to assess whether or not the expected consumer health protection is delivered. On the basis of a review of the information collected through the various appropriate monitoring activities, a decision may be taken to amend the MRM activities implemented or to substitute the option for another one.

MRM activities should be reviewed when new activities or new information (e.g. emerging hazard, virulence of a pathogen, prevalence and concentration in foods, sensitivity of subpopulations, changes in dietary intake patterns) become available.

Industry and other interested parties (e.g. consumers) can suggest the review of MRM options. Evaluation of the success of MRM activities in industry may include reviewing the effectiveness of the food safety control system and its prerequisite programmes, results of product testing, the incidence and nature of product withdrawals/recalls and consumer complaints.

The results of review and the associated actions that risk managers are considering taking, as a consequence of the review, should be made public and communicated to all interested parties.

ANNEX 1

SUGGESTED ELEMENTS TO INCLUDE IN A MICROBIOLOGICAL RISK PROFILE

A risk profile should present, to the extent possible, information on the following.

1. Hazard–food commodity combination(s) of concern:
    *   Hazard(s) of concern.
    *   Description of the food or food product and/or condition of its use with which problems (foodborne illness, trade restrictions) due to this hazard have been associated.
    *   Occurrence of the hazard in the food chain.

2. Description of the public health problem:
    *   Description of the hazard, including key attributes that are the focus of its public health impact (e.g. virulence characteristics, thermal resistance, antimicrobial resistance).
    *   Characteristics of the disease, including:
        –   susceptible populations;
        –   annual incidence rate in humans including, if possible, any differences between age and sex;
        –   outcome of exposure;
        –   severity of clinical manifestations (e.g. case-fatality rate, rate of hospitalization);
        –   nature and frequency of long-term complications;
        –   availability and nature of treatment;
        –   percentage of annual cases attributable to foodborne transmission.
    *   Epidemiology of foodborne disease:
        –   aetiology of foodborne diseases;
        –   characteristics of the foods implicated;
        –   food use and handling that influences transmission of the hazard;
        –   frequency and characteristics of foodborne sporadic cases;
        –   epidemiological data from outbreak investigations.
    *   Regional, seasonal and ethnic differences in the incidence of foodborne illness due to the hazard.
    *   Economic impact or burden of the disease, if readily available:
        –   medical, hospital costs;
        –   working days lost due to illness, etc.

3. Food production, processing, distribution and consumption:
    *   Characteristics of the commodity (commodities) that are involved and that may affect risk management.

- Description of the farm-to-table continuum, including factors that may affect the microbiological safety of the commodity (i.e. primary production, processing, transport, storage, consumer handling practices).
- What is currently known about the risk, how it arises with respect to the commodity's production, processing, transport and consumer handling practices, and who it affects.
- Summary of the extent and effectiveness of current risk management practices, including food safety production/processing control measures, educational programmes, and public health intervention programmes (e.g. vaccines).
- Identification of additional risk mitigation strategies that could be used to control the hazard.

4. Other risk profile elements:
    - The extent of international trade in the food commodity.
    - Existence of regional/international trade agreements and how they may affect the public health impact with respect to the specific hazard/commodity combination(s).
    - Public perceptions of the problem and the risk.
    - Potential public health and economic consequences of establishing Codex MRM guidance document.

5. Risk assessment needs and questions for the risk assessors:
    - Initial assessments of the need and benefits to be gained from requesting an MRA, and the feasibility that such an assessment could be accomplished within the required time frame.
    - If a risk assessment is identified as being needed, recommended questions that should be posed to the risk assessor.

6. Available information and major knowledge gaps provide, to the extent possible, information on the following:
    - Existing national MRAs on the hazard/commodity combination(s) including, if possible:
        - other relevant scientific knowledge and data that would facilitate MRM activities including, if warranted, the conduct of an MRA;
        - existing Codex MRM guidance documents (including existing Codes of hygienic practice and/or Codes of practice);
        - international and/or national governmental and/or industry Codes of hygienic practice and related information (e.g. microbiological criteria) that could be considered in developing a Codex MRM guidance document;
        - sources (organizations, individuals) of information and scientific expertise that could be used in developing a Codex MRM guidance document;
        - areas where major absences of information exist that could hamper MRM activities including, if warranted, the conduct of an MRA.

ANNEX 2

GUIDANCE ON MICROBIOLOGICAL RISK MANAGEMENT METRICS

INTRODUCTION

Three general principles are articulated in the *Recommended International Code of Practice – General Principles of food hygiene* (CAC/RCP 1-1969), its annex "Hazard Analysis and Critical Control Point (HACCP) system and guidelines for its application", and the recently adopted *Principles and Guidelines for the conduct of microbiological risk management* (CAC/GL 63-2007): (i) the stringency of food safety systems should be appropriate for the dual goals of managing risks to public health and ensuring fair practices in the food trade; (ii) the level of control required of a food safety control system should be based on risk and determined using a scientific and transparent approach; and (iii) the performance of a food safety control system should be verifiable. These goals have traditionally been achieved, in part, through the establishment of microbiological criteria (MC), process criteria (PcC) and/or product criteria (PdC). These metrics have provided both a means of articulating the level of stringency expected of a food safety control system and verifying that this level of control is being achieved. However, these traditional risk management tools have generally not been linked directly to a specific level of public health protection. Instead, these metrics have been based on qualitative consideration of the levels of hazards that are "as low as reasonably achievable", a hazard-based approach that does not directly consider the level of control needed to manage a risk to public health. The recent adoption of the "Working Principles for risk analysis for application in the framework of the Codex Alimentarius" and the "Working Principles for risk analysis for food safety for application by governments" has emphasized the goal of Codex Alimentarius to develop risk-based approaches that can more directly and transparently relate the stringency of control measures to achievement of a specified level of public health protection.

A risk management approach based on risk is an important step in improving a food safety system based on science by linking food safety requirements and criteria to the public health problems they are designed to address. Recent advances in microbiological risk assessment (MRA) techniques, such as quantitative microbiological risk assessments (QMRAs), qualitative risk assessments and formalized expert elicitations, are increasingly making it possible to relate the performance of a control measure, a series of control measures or even an entire food safety control system more systematically to the level of control needed to manage a food safety risk. This has been particularly true with QMRA techniques, which allow the impact of different degrees of stringency to be considered quantitatively in relation to predicted public health outcomes. This increased analytical capability has led to a series of new food-safety risk-management metrics, such as the food safety objective (FSO), performance objective (PO), and performance criteria (PC), which are intended to provide a bridge between traditional food safety metrics (i.e. MC, PcC, PdC) and the expected level of public health protection. Such metrics provide a potential means of articulating the level of stringency required of a food safety system at different points in the farm-to-table continuum, thereby providing a means for "operationalizing" the appropriate level of protection (ALOP) concepts envisioned in the WTO SPS Agreement.

As outlined in the main body of this document, the ability to articulate the expected performance of control measures and food safety control systems in terms of the necessary management of public health risks is a critical component of the evolving Codex Alimentarius risk analysis paradigm. While MRA is increasingly used to evaluate the ability of control measures and food safety control systems to achieve a desired degree of public health protection, its application to the development of metrics that can be used to communicate this stringency within an international or national food safety risk management framework is still in its infancy. In particular, the risk assessment tools for linking the establishment of traditional metrics and other guidance for the hygienic manufacture, distribution and consumption of foods to their anticipated public health impact can be complex and not always intuitive. Furthermore, effective risk assessments generally have to consider the variability and uncertainty associated with risk factors, whereas most risk management decisions that are consistent with the legal frameworks underpinning the authority of most competent authorities must ultimately be simplified to a binary criterion (e.g. "acceptable or not acceptable", "safe or unsafe").

SCOPE

The purpose of this annex is to provide guidance to Codex and national governments on the concepts and principles for the development and implementation of microbiological risk management (MRM) metrics, including how risk managers and risk assessors may interact during this process.

The guidance provided by the annex should also prove useful to the food industry and other stakeholders who have the responsibility of devising, validating and implementing control measures that will ensure that, once established, an MRM metric will be achieved on a consistent basis.

It is beyond the scope of this document to consider in detail the risk assessment tools, techniques and mathematical/statistical principles that may be pertinent to the development and implementation of specific metrics for a specific food/hazard.

USE OF THE DOCUMENT

This annex provides general guidance on approaches to the establishment of MRM metrics to relate the level of stringency of control measures or entire food safety control systems more objectively and transparently to the required level of public health protection. The annex also addresses the use of these metrics as a means of communicating and verifying risk management decisions. Recourse to MRM metrics is not always the most appropriate approach to address all food safety management questions. In some cases where a full risk assessment is not available, sound scientific information may be entirely valid and sufficient to inform risk managers, who may decide to implement control measures without directly linking their impact to the public health outcomes. The level of application by competent authorities may vary, taking into account knowledge and availability of scientific information. It is up to the competent authorities to prioritize foods relevant to the countries for considering the application of MRM metrics.

This annex should be used in conjunction with the Codex "Working Principles for risk analysis for application in the framework of the Codex Alimentarius,"[15] *Principles and Guidelines for the conduct of microbiological risk assessment* (CAC/GL 30-1999), *Principles and Guidelines for the conduct of microbiological risk management* (CAC/GL 63-2007), *Working Principles for risk analysis for food safety for application by governments* (CAC/GL 62-2007), "Hazard Analysis and Critical Control Point (HACCP) system and guidelines for its application" (Annex to *Recommended International Code of Practice – General Principles of food hygiene* [CAC/RCP 1-1969]), *Principles for the establishment and application of microbiological criteria for food* (CAC/GL 21-1997) and *Guidelines for the validation of food safety control measures* (CAC/GL 69-2008).

Its application is also dependent on having risk assessment and risk management teams that are familiar with the concepts, tools and limitations of both risk management and risk assessment. Accordingly, it is recommended that the members of such teams use this annex in conjunction with standard references such as the technical information developed by FAO/WHO and Codex Alimentarius. It is recognized that, given the recent elaboration of the MRM metrics concept, there is a need for development of a practical manual to facilitate implementation by countries that have no experience in implementation of these metrics.

PRINCIPLES FOR THE ESTABLISHMENT AND IMPLEMENTATION OF MICROBIOLOGICAL RISK MANAGEMENT METRICS

These principles are in addition to those identified in the "Principles and Guidelines for the conduct of microbiological risk management".

1. The establishment and implementation of MRM metrics should follow a structured approach, with both the risk assessment phase and the subsequent risk management decisions being fully transparent and documented.
2. MRM metrics should be applied only to the extent necessary to protect human life or health and set at a level that is not more trade-restrictive than required to achieve an importing member's ALOP.
3. MRM metrics should be feasible, appropriate for the intended purpose, and applied within a specific food chain context at the appropriate step in that food chain.
4. MRM metrics should be developed and appropriately implemented so they are consistent with the requirements of the regulatory/legal system in which they will be used.

---

[15] Codex Alimentarius Commission, *Procedural Manual.*

RELATIONSHIP BETWEEN VARIOUS RISK MANAGEMENT METRICS

A key food safety responsibility of competent authorities is to articulate the level of control that it expects industry to achieve. One tool commonly used by competent authorities has been the development and use of food safety metrics. The metrics employed by competent authorities have been evolving over time as management of food safety issues has moved from a hazard-based approach to a risk-based approach.

Traditional metrics

Traditional metrics for establishing the stringency of one or more steps in a food safety control system include PdC, PcC and MC.

Product criterion

A PdC specifies a chemical or physical characteristic of a food (e.g. pH, water activity) that, if met, contributes to food safety. Product criteria are used to articulate conditions that will limit growth of a pathogen of concern or will contribute to inactivation, thereby decreasing the potential for risk to increase during subsequent distribution, marketing and preparation. Underlying a PdC is information related to the frequency and level of the contamination in the food and/or raw ingredients that is likely to occur, the effectiveness of the control measure, the sensitivity of the pathogen to the control measure, the conditions of product use, and related parameters that ensure that a product will not have the pathogen at an unacceptable level when the product is consumed. Ideally, each of these factors that determine the effectiveness of a PdC would be transparently considered when the criterion was being established.

Process criterion

A PcC specifies the conditions of treatment that a food must undergo at a specific step in its manufacture to achieve a desired level of control of a microbiological hazard. For example, a milk pasteurization requirement of a heat treatment of 72 °C for 15 seconds specifies the specific time and temperature needed to reduce the levels of *Coxiella burnetii* in milk by 5 logs. Another example would be specifying the times and temperatures for refrigerated storage that are based on preventing the growth of mesophilic pathogenic bacteria such as *Salmonella enterica* in raw meat. Underlying a PcC should be a transparent articulation of the factors that influence the effectiveness of the treatment. For the milk pasteurization example, this would include factors such as the level of the pathogens of concern in raw milk, the thermal resistance among different strains of the micro-organisms, the variation in the ability of the process to deliver the desired heat treatment and the degree of hazard reduction required.

Microbiological criterion

An MC is based on the examination of foods at a specific point in the food chain to determine if the frequency and/or level of a pathogen in a food exceed a pre-established limit (e.g. the microbiological limit associated with a two-class sampling plan). Such microbiological testing can either be employed as a direct control measure (i.e. each lot of food is tested and unsatisfactory lots removed) or, in conjunction with an HACCP plan or other food safety control system, as a periodic means of verifying that a food safety control system is functioning as intended. As a technological and statistically-based tool, an MC requires articulation of the number of samples to be examined, the size of those samples, the method of analysis and its sensitivity, the number of "positives" and/or number of micro-organisms that will result in the lot of food being considered unacceptable or defective (i.e. has a concentration or percentage of contaminated units exceeding the predetermined limit), and the probability that the predetermined limit has not been exceeded. An MC also requires articulation of the actions that are to be taken if the MC is exceeded. The effective use of an MC is dependent on a selection of a sampling plan based on the above parameters to establish the appropriate level of stringency. Because the levels of a pathogen in many foods can change over the course of their manufacture, distribution, marketing and preparation, an MC is generally established at a specific point in the food chain and that MC may not be pertinent at other points. Underlying an MC should be a transparent articulation of the predetermined limit and the rationale for the sampling plan chosen.

Emerging metrics
The increased emphasis on risk analysis as a means for managing food safety concerns has led to increased interest in the development of risk-based metrics that can be more directly related to public health outcomes through a risk assessment process. Three such risk-based metrics that have been defined by the Codex Alimentarius Commission are the FSO, PO and PC. The quantitative aspects of these metrics have been specifically defined by the CAC,[16] but application of metrics that have variations in their quantitative expression may still satisfy the goals and principles presented in this annex.

Food safety objective
The FSO is a metric articulating the maximum frequency and/or concentration of a pathogen in a food at the time of consumption that provides or contributes to the ALOP. An FSO can be an important component of a risk-based system of food safety. By setting an FSO, competent authorities articulate a risk-based limit that should be achieved operationally within the food chain, while providing flexibility for different production, manufacturing, distribution, marketing and preparation approaches.

Because of the link between FSO and ALOP, FSOs are established only by national competent authorities. Codex can help in establishing FSOs, for instance, through recommendations based on national or international microbiological risk assessments. Food safety objectives should be given effect by actions at earlier stages in the food chain by the competent authority and/or the individual food business operator (e.g. food manufacturer) setting POs, PCs or MCs, as appropriate.

There are two approaches to establishing an FSO. One is based on an analysis of the public health data and epidemiological surveys. The other is based on analysis of data on the level and/or frequency of a hazard in a food to develop a risk characterization curve linking hazard levels to disease incidence. If such a curve is available for a given hazard, it can be a helpful basis for relating the FSO to the ALOP.

[16] Codex Alimentarius Commission, *Procedural Manual*.

In countries, FSOs can be used:

- to express the ALOP (whether explicit or implicit) as a more useful parameter for the industry and other interested parties;
- to encourage change in industry food-safety control systems, or in the behaviour of consumers, in order to enhance food safety;
- for communication to parties involved in food trade;
- as a performance target for entire food chains to enable industry to design its operational food safety control system (through establishing appropriate POs, PCs and other control measures and interaction between the participants of the food chain in question).

Because the FSO relates to the time of consumption, it is unlikely that a competent authority would set an FSO as a regulatory metric owing to the unverifiable nature of this point in the food chain.

FSOs may not be universal among all countries and may need to take into account regional differences.

Performance objective

The articulation of a PO by a risk manager provides an operational (see below) risk-based limit in a food at a specific point in the food chain, i.e. the maximum frequency and/or concentration of a microbiological hazard in a food at that point in the food chain that should not be exceeded if one is to have confidence that the FSO or ALOP will be maintained. Because a PO is conceptually linked to the FSO and ALOP, the impact of the steps in the food chain both before and subsequent to the PO should be considered in setting its value. For example, consider a PO for bottled water that specifies that the level of *Salmonella* after a microbiocidal treatment must be less than $-2.0 \log_{10}$ CFU/ml. This would require consideration of the level of *Salmonella* in the incoming untreated water over a period of time, as well as the effectiveness of the microbiocidal treatment to reduce that level of contamination. The establishment of the PO in relation to controlling the overall risk would also have to consider any post-treatment increases in the level of surviving *Salmonella* or recontamination of the product prior to consumption.

The frequency and/or concentration of a hazard at individual steps throughout the food chain can differ substantially from the FSO. Therefore, the following generic guidelines should apply:

- If the food is likely to support the growth of a microbial hazard between the point of the PO and consumption, then the PO will necessarily have to be more stringent than the FSO. The difference in stringency will depend on the magnitude of the increase in levels expected.
- If it can be demonstrated and validated that the level of the hazard will decrease after the point of the PO (e.g. cooking by the final consumer), the PO may be less stringent than the FSO. By basing a PO on the FSO, the frequency of cross-contamination could also be factored into the control strategy. For example, establishing a PO for frequency of *Salmonella* contamination of raw poultry

earlier in the food chain would contribute to a reduction of illness associated with poultry mediated cross-contamination in the steps to follow.

- If the frequency and/or concentration of the hazard is not likely to increase or decrease between the point of the PO and consumption, then the PO and the FSO will be the same.

An MRA can assist in determining the relationship between a PO and an FSO. An MRA can also provide the risk manager with knowledge of hazard levels possibly occurring at specific steps in the chain and of issues regarding the feasibility in practice to comply with a proposed PO/FSO. In designing its food safety control system such that the PO (set by a competent authority or the individual food business) and the FSO (set by a competent authority) are met, the individual food business will have to make provisions reflecting its ability to consistently meet these standards in operational practice, including consideration of a margin of safety.

The individual food business may find it beneficial to establish its own POs. These POs should normally not be universally common and should take into account the position of the business within the food chain, the various conditions at the subsequent steps in the food chain (probability and extent of pathogen growth under specified storage and transport conditions, shelf-life, etc.) and the intended use of the end products (domestic consumer handling, etc.). Although compliance with POs is not always verified by analytical means, verifying that a PO is being consistently met can be achieved by measures such as:

- monitoring and recording of pertinent validated control measures, including establishment of a statistically based, validated MC for end products;
- monitoring programmes on the prevalence of a microbial hazard in a food (especially relevant for POs established by competent authorities).

Performance criterion

A PC articulates an outcome that should be achieved by a control measure or a series or a combination of control measures. Generally, a PC is used in conjunction with a microbiocidal (e.g. thermal treatment, antimicrobial rinse) or microbiostatic (e.g. refrigeration, water activity reduction) control measure. A PC for a microbiocidal control measure expresses the desired reduction of the microbial population that occurs during the application of the control measure (e.g. 5-log reduction in the levels of *L. monocytogenes*). A PC for a microbiostatic control measure expresses the maximum increase in the microbial population that is acceptable under the various conditions during which the measure is applied (e.g. less than a 1-log increase in *L. monocytogenes* during refrigerated distribution of a ready-to-eat food). In many instances, the PC describes the outcome that is needed in order to achieve a PO at a specified point in the food chain. There are a number of factors that would have to be considered in reaching a decision on the value of a PC, such as the variability of pathogen levels in raw ingredients or the variability associated with a processing technology.

PCs are generally set by individual food businesses. A PC may be set by national governments for a specific control measure, where its application by industry is generally uniform and/or as advice to food businesses that are not capable of establishing PCs themselves.

Such PCs are often translated by industry or sometimes by competent authorities into a PcC or a PdC. For example, if a PC indicated that a heat treatment should provide a 5-log reduction of a hazard, then the corresponding process criteria would stipulate the specific time and temperature combination(s) that would be needed to achieve the PC. Similarly, if a PC required that an acidification treatment of a food reduce the rate of growth of a hazard to less than 1-log in two weeks, then the PdC would be the specific acid concentration and pH that would be needed to achieve the PC. The concepts of process criteria and product criteria have been long recognized and used by industry and competent authorities.

INTEGRATION OF MICROBIOLOGICAL RISK MANAGEMENT METRICS WITHIN A FOOD SAFETY CONTROL SYSTEM

A key concept underlying the *Recommended International Code of Practice – General Principles of food hygiene* (CAC/RCP 1-1969) is that key control measures must be integrated into a "farm-to-table" food safety control system in order to produce consistently a food product that achieves the desired level of public health protection (i.e. the ALOP). Because the purpose of establishing and implementing MRM metrics is to articulate and verify, in an objective and transparent manner as far as possible, the stringency of control measures needed to achieve a specific level of public health protection, it is likely that metrics may be implemented at multiple points along the food chain. A key to understanding the development of such metrics is an appreciation that the metrics implemented along a food chain should be interconnected. There are two types of interconnections. The first is the relationship among different types of MRM metrics at a specific step in the food chain. The second is that, ideally, metrics implemented along the food chain would be integrated such that the establishment of a metric at one point in the food chain can be related to the outcome at another and ultimately to the desired public health outcome.

The PO is likely to be the primary risk-based metric used by competent authorities to articulate the level of control (i.e. frequency and/or concentration) of a hazard at a specified point in the food chain. Once articulated, the PO in conjunction with additional information can be used to derive other MRM metrics. As a simplified example, consider a PO after a heat treatment of a food is a *Salmonella* concentration of ≤ -4.0 $\log_{10}$ (CFU/g). If the maximum level of *Salmonella* likely to occur in the food prior to heating is $+1.0$ $\log_{10}$ (CFU/g), then the PC for this step would be a 5-log reduction. The PC value in conjunction with information on the thermal resistance of *Salmonella* could be used to articulate specific time/temperature combinations (i.e. PcC values) that would achieve the 5-log reduction. The same concept underpins the relationship between a PO and an MC. In this instance, the MC is used to verify that a PO is not being exceeded. The PO value in conjunction with information on the likely variance of the pathogen's presence and the level of confidence required by the risk managers is used to develop a sampling plan and decision criteria associated with an MC. In general, the microbiological limit associated with an MC will have to be more stringent than its corresponding PO to take into account the degree of confidence required that the food does not exceed a PO. It is also important for risk managers to appreciate that, in the absence of an explicit PO, the establishment of MRM metrics such as a PC, PcC, PdC or MC, in combination with the additional information described above, will allow the PO for a control measure to be inferred.

As indicated earlier, the establishment of MRM metrics at different points along the food chain should take into account the changes in the frequency and/or concentration of a hazard that occur during a specific segment of the food safety control system if the desired level of overall control is to be achieved. Recent advances in MRA are increasingly allowing MRM metrics at different points to be related to each other and to the overall level of protection achieved by the food safety control system. The ability to relate PO and other metrics implemented at intermediate steps in the food chain to a PO or FSO established by a competent authority would be a useful tool for industry to design and verify that their control measures are achieving the desired level of control.

The integration of MRM metrics both at a specific point in the food chain and between points in the food chain will require the availability of subject matter experts and appropriate models and data pertinent to the food product and the processes and ingredients used in its manufacture, distribution and marketing.

KEY RISK ASSESSMENT CONCEPTS RELATED TO THE DEVELOPMENT AND USE OF MICROBIOLOGICAL RISK MANAGEMENT METRICS

An integral part of the development of food safety metrics is a consideration of the variability inherent in the food ingredients, the control measures and ultimately the food that determine the range of results that can be expected when a food safety control system is functioning as intended. Likewise, any uncertainties associated with the parameters affecting the food safety control system should be considered when establishing an integrated set of food safety risk management metrics. Both variability and uncertainty can be evaluated using QMRA techniques in conjunction with an appropriately designed risk assessment, providing a tool for formally evaluating and documenting how these important attributes were considered in the decision-making process.

One of the challenges in establishing and integrating the risk management metrics described above is translating the results of a risk assessment into a set of simple limits that can be communicated and implemented. This reflects the fact that QMRAs are often based on probabilistic models that typically employ unbounded distributions (e.g. log-normal distributions for microbial populations) that have no maximum value. Thus, there is calculable probability that a metric could be exceeded when the control measure or food safety control system is functioning as intended. For example, if a control measure was designed to ensure that the level of bacteria at an intermediate processing step had a geometric mean of $\log_{10}$ (CFU/g) = 3.0 and a standard deviation of 0.3 and was operating as intended, it would be expected that approximately one serving in 200 would have $\log_{10}$ (CFU/g) = 4.0 and approximately one serving in 1 000 000 would have $\log_{10}$ (CFU/g) = 4.7.

The implication of this concept is a characteristic inherent to the use of MRM metrics. Using the example above, if it is assumed that an MC has been set by the risk manager to have a degree of confidence that a lot having servings that exceeded $\log_{10}$ (CFU/g) = 4.5 would be detected and rejected, any occasion when the MC is exceeded will be considered a loss of control, even though there is a small possibility that the system may be working as intended. MRM metrics will have to be made "operational" by deciding what portion of a potentially open-ended distribution for an "under control" control measure will be considered as exceeding the limit and the degree of confidence, such that any serving of food exceeding that value is rejected (e.g. 95 percent confidence that 99 percent of servings of a ready-to-eat food have fewer than 1 *Salmonella* per 100 g). While there are techniques that can be used to include some consideration of distributions within risk management decisions and verification criteria (e.g. three-class attribute sampling plans), a series of operational assumptions will be required for any MRM metric. A critical component of establishing such a metric is ensuring that the underlying assumptions are understood by the risk managers and interested parties.

AN EXAMPLE OF A PROCESS FOR ESTABLISHING AND IMPLEMENTING MICROBIOLOGICAL RISK MANAGEMENT METRICS

While the development of MRM metrics should follow a structured approach, the processes and procedures put into place by competent authorities for the establishment of integrated MRM metrics should be highly flexible in relation to what metric is initially used to begin relating the performance of the food safety control system to its public health outcomes. The process can begin with an articulation of a level of disease control that must be achieved (i.e. ALOP), the exposure level that should not be exceeded at consumption (i.e. FSO), a level of control of a hazard that must be achieved at a specific point in the food chain (i.e. PO), a required processing outcome at a specific step (i.e. PC), an MC, etc.

When development of an MRM metric is being considered, there will probably be a need for close communication and mutual understanding between risk assessors and risk managers. The development of specific MRM metrics will probably require the formation of appropriate risk analysis teams consisting of appropriate subject-matter experts. Scientific advice and data for specific hazard/food applications should be acquired from appropriate scientific organizations, competent authorities, process control experts or related sources of scientific expertise.

Where appropriate, risk assessors and risk managers may wish to consider the following protocol, or some variation thereof, as a means of ensuring the principles for MRM lead to transparent, informed decisions.

a) The risk managers commission the risk assessors to develop a risk assessment or other suitable scientific analysis that can inform the possible development of MRM metrics.

b) The risk managers, after consultation with the risk assessors, select one or more sites along the food chain for the product where a risk management metric may be pertinent, useful and practical.

c) The risk assessors use the risk assessment to evaluate how different values for the MRM metric being considered are related to the consumers' exposure and the subsequent public health outcomes. Whenever feasible, the risk assessors should provide the risk managers with an array of values for potential MRM metrics, information on uncertainty that may indicate a need for margins of safety and the corresponding level of protection expected if implemented.

d) The risk assessors use the risk assessment and related tools to ensure that the MRM metrics being considered by the risk manager are consistent with one another, appropriately taking into account the increases and decreases in hazard levels that may occur during that portion of the food chain.

e) The risk managers evaluate the practical feasibility of achieving the specific level of stringency through implementation of the metric being considered, including consideration of how to verify that the MRM metric is effectively met.

f) Risk assessors provide advice on the public health implications of non-compliance with a metric being considered.

g) The risk manager selects the MRM metrics to be implemented, their level of stringency, and the strategy for their implementation.

h) At the request of the risk managers, the risk assessors calculate additional MRM metrics that may be derived or inferred from the decision in Step g).

i) Risk managers implement, in conjunction with industry, the risk management metrics.

j) Risk managers review implemented MRM metrics for the degree of implementation, efficacy and ongoing relevance. The criteria for review should be decided when the MRM metrics are initially implemented. For instance, review can be periodic and/or may also be triggered by other factors such as new scientific insights, changes in public health policy, or changes in the food chain context in which the metrics are applied.

GENERAL STANDARD FOR IRRADIATED FOODS

CODEX STAN 106-1983

1. SCOPE

This standard applies to foods processed by ionizing radiation that is used in conjunction with applicable hygienic codes, food standards and transportation codes. It does not apply to foods exposed to doses imparted by measuring instruments used for inspection purposes.

2. GENERAL REQUIREMENTS FOR THE PROCESS

2.1 Radiation sources

The following types of ionizing radiation may be used:

a) gamma rays from the radionuclides ^{60}Co or ^{137}Cs;

b) X-rays generated from machine sources operated at or below an energy level of 5 MeV;

c) electrons generated from machine sources operated at or below an energy level of 10 MeV.

2.2 Absorbed dose

For the irradiation of any food, the minimum absorbed dose should be sufficient to achieve the technological purpose and the maximum absorbed dose should be less than that which would compromise consumer safety, wholesomeness or would adversely affect structural integrity, functional properties, or sensory attributes. The maximum absorbed dose delivered to a food should not exceed 10 kGy, except when necessary to achieve a legitimate technological purpose.[1]

2.3 Facilities and control of the process

2.3.1 Radiation treatment of foods should be carried out in facilities licensed and registered for this purpose by the competent authority.

2.3.2 The facilities shall be designed to meet the requirements of safety, efficacy and good hygienic practices of food processing.

2.3.3 The facilities should be staffed by adequate, trained and competent personnel.

2.3.4 Control of the process within the facility should include the keeping of adequate records including quantitative dosimetry.

---

[1] *High dose irradiation: wholesomeness of food irradiated with doses above 10 kGy,* Report of a Joint FAO/IAEA/WHO Study Group, Technical Report Series No. 890 WHO. Geneva, Switzerland, 1999; *Safety and nutritional adequacy of irradiated foods,* WHO, Geneva, Switzerland, 1994; and *Wholesomeness of irradiated food,* Report of Joint FAO/IAEA/ WHO Expert Committee, Technical Report Series No. 659, WHO, Geneva, Switzerland, 1981.

Formerly CAC/RS-1979. Adopted 1983. Revision 2003.

2.3.5   Facilities and records should be open to inspection by appropriate authorities.

2.3.6   Control should be carried out in accordance with the *Recommended International Code of Practice for radiation processing of food* (CAC/RCP 19-1979).

3.   HYGIENE OF IRRADIATED FOODS

3.1   The irradiated food should be prepared, processed and transported hygienically in accordance with the provisions of the *Recommended International Code of Practice – General Principles of food hygiene* (CAC/RCP 1-1969), including the application of the seven principles of the Hazard Analysis and Critical Control Point (HACCP) system where applicable for food safety purposes. Where appropriate, the technical requirements for the raw materials and end product should comply with applicable hygienic codes, food standards, and transportation codes.

3.2   Any relevant national public health requirement affecting microbiological safety and nutritional adequacy applicable in the country in which the food is sold should be observed.

4.   TECHNOLOGICAL REQUIREMENTS

4.1   **General requirement**
The irradiation of food is justified only when it fulfils a technological requirement and/or is beneficial for the protection of consumer health. It should not be used as a substitute for good hygienic and good manufacturing practices or good agricultural practices.

4.2   **Food quality and packaging requirements**
The doses applied shall be commensurate with the technological and public health purposes to be achieved and shall be in accordance with good radiation processing practice. Foods to be irradiated and their packaging materials shall be of suitable quality, acceptable hygienic condition and appropriate for this purpose and shall be handled, before and after irradiation, according to good manufacturing practices, taking into account the particular requirements of the technology of the process.

5.   RE-IRRADIATION

5.1   Except for foods with low moisture content (cereals, pulses, dehydrated foods and other such commodities) irradiated for the purpose of controlling insect reinfestation, foods irradiated in accordance with Sections 2 and 4 of this standard should not be re-irradiated.

5.2   For the purpose of this standard, food is not considered as having been re-irradiated when: (a) the irradiated food is prepared from materials that have been irradiated at low dose levels for purposes other than food safety, e.g. quarantine control, prevention of sprouting of roots and tubers; (b) the food, containing less than 5 percent of irradiated ingredient, is irradiated; or (c) the full dose of ionizing radiation required to achieve the desired effect is applied to the food in more than one increment as part of processing for a specific technological purpose.

5.3   The cumulative maximum absorbed dose delivered to a food should not exceed 10 kGy as a result of re-irradiation except when it is necessary to achieve a legitimate technological purpose, and should not compromise consumer safety or wholesomeness of the food.

6. LABELLING

6.1   Inventory control
For irradiated foods, whether prepackaged or not, the relevant shipping documents shall give appropriate information to identify the registered facility that has irradiated the food, the date(s) of treatment, irradiation dose and lot identification.

6.2   Prepackaged foods intended for direct consumption
The labelling of prepackaged irradiated foods should indicate the treatment and in all aspects should be in accordance with the relevant provisions of the *General Standard for the labelling of prepackaged foods* (CODEX STAN 1-1985).

6.3   Foods in bulk containers
The declaration of the fact of irradiation should be made clear on the relevant shipping documents. In the case of products sold in bulk to the ultimate consumer, the international logo and the words "irradiated" or "treated with ionizing radiation" should appear together with the name of the product on the container in which products are placed.

6.4   Post-irradiation verification
When required and where applicable, analytical methods for the detection of irradiated foods may be used to enforce authorization and labelling requirements. The analytical methods used should be those adopted by the Codex Commission.

RECOMMENDED INTERNATIONAL CODE OF PRACTICE FOR RADIATION PROCESSING OF FOOD

CAC/RCP 19-1979

INTRODUCTION

Food irradiation is the processing of food products by ionizing radiation in order to, among other things, control foodborne pathogens, reduce microbial load and insect infestation, inhibit the germination of root crops, and extend the durable life of perishable produce. Many countries use industrial irradiators for processing food products for commercial purposes.

The regulatory control of food irradiation should take into consideration the *General Standard for irradiated foods* (CODEX STAN 106-1983) and this Code.

The purpose of regulatory control of irradiated food products should be:
a)   to ensure that radiation processing of food products is implemented safely and correctly, in accordance with all relevant Codex Standards and Codes of hygienic practice;
b)   to establish a system of documentation to accompany irradiated food products, so that the fact of irradiation can be taken into account during subsequent handling, storage and marketing; and
c)   to ensure that irradiated food products that enter into international trade conform to acceptable standards of radiation processing and are correctly labelled.

The purpose of this Code is to provide principles for the processing of food products with ionizing radiation that are consistent with relevant Codex Standards and Codes of hygienic practice. Food irradiation may be incorporated as part of a Hazard Analysis and Critical Control Point (HACCP) plan where applicable; but an HACCP plan is not required for the use of radiation processing of food processed for purposes other than for food safety. The provisions of this Code will provide guidance to the radiation processor to apply the HACCP system, as recommended in the *Recommended International Code of Practice – General Principles of food hygiene* (CAC/RCP 1-1969), where applicable for food safety purposes, to foods processed by ionizing radiation.

1.   OBJECTIVES

This *Recommended International Code of Practice for radiation processing of food* identifies the essential practices to be implemented to achieve effective radiation processing of food products in a manner that maintains quality and yields food products that are safe and suitable for consumption.

Adopted in 1997. Revision 2003.

2. SCOPE, USE AND DEFINITIONS

2.1 **Scope**

This Code is concerned with food products processed by gamma rays, X-rays or accelerated electrons for the purpose of, among other things, control of foodborne pathogens, reduction of microbial load and insect infestation, inhibition of the germination of root crops, and extension of durable life for perishable foods.

This Code covers the requirements of the irradiation process in a facility; it also considers other aspects of the process, such as primary production and/or harvesting, post-harvest treatment, storage and shipment, packaging, irradiation, labelling, post-irradiation storage and handling, and training.[1]

2.2 **Use**

The *Recommended International Code of Practice – General Principles of food hygiene* (CAC/RCP 1-1969,) and its annex on application of the HACCP system, as well as other relevant Codex Standards and Codes of hygienic practice should be used with this document. Of particular relevance are the *General Standard for irradiated foods* (CODEX STAN 106-1983) and the *General Standard for the labelling of prepackaged foods* (CODEX STAN 1-1985).

2.3 **Definitions**

For purposes of this Code, the terms below are defined as follows:

Food irradiation Processing of food products by ionizing radiation, specifically gamma rays, X-rays or accelerated electrons as specified in the *General Standard for irradiated foods* (CODEX STAN 106-1983).

Irradiated food Food products processed by ionizing radiation in accordance with the *General Standard for irradiated foods* (CODEX STAN 106-1983). Such food is subject to all relevant standards, codes and regulations applicable to the non-irradiated counterpart.

Dosimetry The measurement of the absorbed dose of radiation at a particular point in a given absorbing medium.

Dose (absorbed) The absorbed dose, sometimes referred to simply as "dose", is the amount of energy absorbed per unit mass of irradiated food product.

Dose uniformity ratio The ratio of maximum to minimum absorbed dose in the production lot.

Dose distribution The spatial variation in absorbed dose throughout the production lot with extreme values being the maximum absorbed dose and the minimum absorbed dose.

Dose limit The minimum or maximum radiation dose absorbed by a food product prescribed in regulations as required for technological reasons. Such dose limits

---

[1] Codes of good irradiation practice, compilations of technical data for the authorization and control of the irradiation of several food classes and also training manuals for facility operators and control officials have been produced by the International Consultative Group on Food Irradiation (ICGFI), available through the International Atomic Energy Agency, PO Box 100, A-1400 Vienna, Austria.

are expressed as ranges or as single lower or upper values (i.e. no part of the food product shall absorb less than or more than a specified amount).

3. PRE-IRRADIATION TREATMENT

3.1 Primary production and/or harvesting

Primary food products intended for radiation processing should comply with the *Recommended International Code of Practice – General Principles of food hygiene* (CAC/RCP 1-1969) with reference to the hygienic requirements as well as other relevant Codex Standards and Codes of practice for primary production and/or harvesting, which ensure that food is safe and suitable for human consumption.

3.2 Handling, storage and transport

The intent to process food products by irradiation poses no unique requirements regarding handling, storage and transport of the food products prior to and subsequent to irradiation. All stages of the processing, i.e. pre-irradiation, irradiation and post-irradiation, should be in accordance with good manufacturing practices to maximize quality, to minimize contamination, and, if packaged, to maintain package integrity.

Radiation is applied to food products in forms in which they are normally prepared for processing, commercially traded or otherwise used. Food intended for radiation processing should conform to handling, storage and transport requirements of the *Recommended International Code of Practice – General Principles of food hygiene* (CAC/RCP 1-1969) as well as relevant Codex Standards and Codes of practice for specific food products.

4. PACKAGING

In general, in order to avoid contamination or infestation after irradiation, food products should be packaged in materials that provide an effective barrier to re-contamination and re-infestation. Packaging must also meet the requirements of the importing country.

The size and shape of containers that may be used for irradiation are determined, in part, by the operating characteristics of the irradiation facility. These characteristics include the product transport systems and the irradiation source, as they affect the dose distribution within the container.

5. ESTABLISHMENT: DESIGN, FACILITIES AND CONTROL

Authorization of a facility to irradiate food is granting approval to a facility licensed for radiation processing in general to irradiate food products. Authorization may be general in nature or issued for specific classes or groups of food products.

Facilities that carry out irradiation of food products should meet appropriate standards of occupational safety and good hygiene conditions, including:

- regulations regarding design, construction and operation of radiation facilities;
- *Recommended International Code of Practice – General Principles of food hygiene* (CAC/RCP 1-1969);
- *General Standard for irradiated foods* (CODEX STAN 106-1983) and this Code.

5.1 Design and layout

This section is concerned with the areas in which food products are stored and irradiated. Prevention of contamination requires that all measures be taken to avoid direct or indirect contact of the food product with sources of potential contamination and to minimize growth of micro-organisms.

Irradiation establishments are laid out to provide storage for irradiated and non-irradiated food products (under ambient, refrigerated and/or freezing temperature conditions), an irradiator, and the normal accommodation and infrastructure for staff and plant services, including record maintenance. In order to achieve inventory control, there should be provision in both the design and operation of the establishment to keep irradiated and non-irradiated food products separate. This separation can be accomplished by controlled single-direction movement of the food products through the plant and by separated storage areas for irradiated and non-irradiated food products.

Radiation facilities must be designed to provide an absorbed dose in the food product within minimum and maximum limits in accordance with process specifications and government regulatory requirements. For economic and technical reasons (e.g. maintaining product quality), various techniques are used to minimize the ratio, which is termed the dose uniformity ratio.

The following factors largely govern the selection of irradiator design:
a) Means of transporting food products: The mechanical design of the irradiation and transport systems, including the source-to-product geometry in a given process, as required by the form of the product, e.g. bulk or packaged, and its properties.
b) Range of doses: The range of doses needed to process a wide variety of products for various applications.
c) Throughput: The amount of product to be processed within a defined period of time.
d) Reliability: The property of providing correct performance as needed.
e) Safety systems: The systems intended to protect operating personnel from hazards posed by radiation.
f) Compliance: The adherence to good manufacturing practices and relevant government regulations.
g) Capital and operational costs: The basic economic considerations necessary for sustainable operation.

5.2   Radiation sources
As described in the *General Standard for irradiated foods* (CODEX STAN 106-1983), the following sources of ionizing radiation may be used in food irradiation:
a)   gamma rays from radionuclides ^{60}Co or ^{137}Cs;
b)   X-rays generated from machine sources operated at or below an energy level of 5 MeV; and
c)   electrons generated from machine sources operated at or below an energy level of 10 MeV.

5.3   Control of operation

5.3.1   **Legislation**
Food processing establishments are constructed and operated in accordance with regulatory requirements in order to ensure safety of the processed foods for consumption and occupational safety of the plant personnel and the environment. A food irradiation facility, like any other food processing plant, is also subject to such regulation and should be designed, constructed and operated in compliance with relevant regulations.

5.3.2   **Requirements for staff**
The staff at an irradiation facility is subject to relevant sections of the *Recommended International Code of Practice – General Principles of food hygiene* (CAC/RCP 1-1969) for personal hygiene recommendations and to the *General Standard for irradiated foods* (CODEX STAN 106-1983) for recommendations regarding the need for adequate, trained and competent personnel.[2]

5.3.3   **Requirements for process control**
Requirements for process control are included in the *General Standard for irradiated foods* (CODEX STAN 106-1983). Measuring the dose and monitoring of the physical parameters of the process are essential for process control. The need for adequate record-keeping, including records of quantitative dosimetry, is emphasized in the General Standard. As for other physical methods of food processing, records are essential means for the regulatory control of processing by ionizing radiation. Evidence for correct processing, including adherence to any legal or technological dose limits, depends on the maintenance of full and accurate records by the irradiation facility. The facility's records link all the information from several sources to the irradiated food products. Such records enable verification of the irradiation process and should be kept.

5.3.4   **Control of applied dose**
The effectiveness of the irradiation process depends on proper application of the dose and its measurement. Dose distribution measurements should be carried out

---

[2]   Training manuals for facility operators and control officials have been produced by the ICGFI, available through the International Atomic Energy Agency, PO Box 100, A-1400 Vienna, Austria. Through its Food Irradiation Process Control School, the ICGFI provides such training.

to characterize the process for each food product; and thereafter dosimeters should be used routinely to monitor correct execution of the process in accordance with internationally accepted procedures.[3]

For certain public health or quarantine applications, there may be specific requirements to regulate the minimum absorbed dose in order to ensure that the desired technological effect is achieved.

5.3.5   **Product and inventory control**
An adequate system should be in place so that specific consignments of food products can be traced back both to the irradiation facility and the source from which they were received for processing.

Plant design and administrative procedures should ensure that it is impossible to mix irradiated and non-irradiated food products. Incoming products should be logged and given a code number to identify the packages at each step in their path through the irradiation plant. All relevant parameters such as date, time, source strength, minimum and maximum dose, temperature, etc. should be logged against the code number of the product.

It is not possible to distinguish irradiated from non-irradiated product by visual inspection. Therefore, it is essential that appropriate means, such as physical barriers, be employed for keeping the irradiated and non-irradiated product separate. Affixing a colour change indicator label on each package, where applicable, provides another means of distinguishing irradiated and non-irradiated product.

6.   IRRADIATION

6.1   General
Refer to the *General Standard for irradiated foods* (CODEX-STAN 106-1983).

6.2   Process determination
It is important that all steps in the determination of process procedures are documented to:
a)   ensure that the application of the process complies with relevant regulatory requirements;
b)   establish a clear statement for the technological objectives of the process;
c)   estimate the dose range to be applied to achieve the technological objective based on appropriate knowledge of the food product;
d)   demonstrate that irradiation of test samples has been carried out to confirm the estimated dose range under practical production conditions;
e)   ensure that it is possible to meet the technological requirements, e.g. dose range and effectiveness of treatment, under practical production conditions; and
f)   establish the process parameters under practical production conditions.

---

[3] Such procedures are specified, for example, by ASTM International in its annual handbooks.

6.3   Dosimetry

Successful radiation processing practice depends on the ability of the processor to measure the absorbed dose delivered to each point in the food product and in the production lot.

Various techniques for dosimetry pertinent to radionuclide and machine sources are available for measuring absorbed dose in a quantitative manner. Relevant ISO/ASTM standard practices and guides for dosimety in food irradiation facilities have been developed and should be consulted.[4]

In order to implement these irradiation practices, facilities should be adequately staffed by competent personnel trained in dosimetry and its application in radiation processing.

The calibration of the dosimetry system used in radiation processing should be traceable (i.e. calibrated) to national and international standards.

6.4   Dosimetry systems

Dosimeters are devices that are capable of providing a quantitative and reproducible measurement of dose through a change in one or more of the physical properties of the dosimeters in response to exposure to ionizing radiation energy. A dosimetry system consists of dosimeters, measurement instruments and their associated reference standards, and procedures for the system's use. Selection of an appropriate dosimetry system for radiation processing of food will depend on a variety of factors, including the dose range needed to achieve a particular technological objective, cost, availability, and ease of use. A variety of dosimetry systems are available.[5]

6.5   Dosimetry and process control

In food irradiation, the key quantity that governs the process is the absorbed dose. It is influenced by various parameters, such as: radiation source type, strength and geometry; conveyor speed or dwell time; food product density and loading configuration; and carrier size and shape.[6] Their overall influence on dose distribution must be taken into account to ensure that the intended technological objective is achieved throughout the production lot.

The application of radiation processing is mainly governed by the minimum absorbed dose achieved in the dose distribution within a given product. If the required minimum is not applied, the intended technical effect may not be achieved (e.g. sprout inhibition,

---

[4] ISO/ASTM 51204 – *Standard practice for dosimetry in gamma irradiation facilities for food processing*; ISO/ASTM 51431 – *Practice for dosimetry in electron beam and X-ray (bremsstrahlung) irradiation facilities for food processing*; ISO/ASTM 51261 – *Guide for selection and calibration of dosimetry systems for radiation processing*.

[5] ISO/ASTM 51261 – *Guide for selection and calibration of dosimetry systems for radiation processing*.

[6] ISO/ASTM 51204 – *Standard practice for dosimetry in gamma irradiation facilities for food processing* and ISO/ASTM 51431 – *Practice for dosimetry in electron beam and X-ray (bremsstrahlung) irradiation facilities for food processing*.

pathogen reduction). There are also situations where the application of too high a dose would impair the quality of the treated food (e.g. off flavours or odours).[7]

6.6 Records of irradiation

Radiation processors should maintain adequate records showing the food processed, identifying marks if packaged or, if not, the shipping details, the bulk density of the food, the dosimetry results, including the type of dosimeters used and details of their calibration, the date of irradiation and the type of radiation source. All documentation should be available to authorized personnel and accessible for a period of time established by food control authorities.

6.7 Control of hazards

Controls of microbiological hazards are described in the *Recommended International Code of Practice – General Principles of food hygiene* (CAC/RCP 1-1969).

The radiation processor should apply HACCP principles, as described in the "Hazard Analysis Critical Control Point (HACCP) system and guidelines for its application", as appropriate. In the overall HACCP context, irradiation is a means of reducing hazards associated with infectious parasites and microbial contamination of foods and may be used as a method of control.

7. POST-IRRADIATION STORAGE AND HANDLING

Refer to the *Recommended International Code of Practice – General Principles of food hygiene* (CAC/RCP 1-1969) for general storage and handling guidance.

8. LABELLING

The *General Standard for irradiated foods* (CODEX STAN 106-1983) and the *General Standard for the labelling of prepackaged foods* (CODEX STAN 1-1985) contain provisions for labelling of irradiated foods, including the internationally recognized symbol (logo) and the inclusion of information in shipping documents, and for the labelling of prepackaged irradiated foods, respectively. All food labelling must meet any additional requirements established by the competent authorities.

---

[7] Codes of good irradiation practice and compilations of technical data for the authorization and control of the irradiation of several food classes have been produced by the ICGFI, available through the International Atomic Energy Agency, PO Box 100, A-1400 Vienna, Austria.

GUIDELINES ON THE APPLICATION OF GENERAL PRINCIPLES OF FOOD HYGIENE TO THE CONTROL OF *LISTERIA MONOCYTOGENES* IN FOODS

CAC/GL 61-2007

Adopted in 2007. Annexes 2 and 3 adopted in 2009.

GUIDELINES ON THE APPLICATION OF GENERAL PRINCIPLES OF FOOD HYGIENE TO THE CONTROL OF *LISTERIA MONOCYTOGENES* IN FOODS

CAC/GL 61-2007

INTRODUCTION

Listeria (L.) monocytogenes is a Gram-positive bacterium that occurs widely in both agricultural (soil, vegetation, silage, faecal material, sewage, water), aquacultural and food-processing environments. *L. monocytogenes* is a transitory resident of the intestinal tract in humans, with 2–10 percent of the general population being carriers of the micro-organism without any apparent health consequences.[1] In comparison with other non-spore-forming, foodborne pathogenic bacteria (e.g. *Salmonella* spp., enterohaemorrhagic Escherichia coli), *L. monocytogenes* is resistant to various environmental conditions such as high salt or acidity. *L. monocytogenes* grows at low oxygen conditions and refrigeration temperatures, and survives for long periods in the environment, on foods, in the processing plant, and in the household refrigerator. Although frequently present in raw foods of both plant and animal origin, sporadic cases or outbreaks of listeriosis are generally associated with ready-to-eat, refrigerated foods, and often involve the post-processing recontamination of cooked foods.

L. monocytogenes has been isolated from foods such as raw vegetables, raw and pasteurized fluid milk, cheeses (particularly soft-ripened varieties), ice cream, butter, fermented raw-meat sausages, raw and cooked poultry, raw and processed meats (all types) and raw, preserved and smoked fish. Even when *L. monocytogenes* is initially present at a low level in a contaminated food, the micro-organism may multiply during storage in foods that support growth, even at refrigeration temperatures.

L. monocytogenes causes invasive listeriosis, wherein the micro-organism penetrates the lining of the gastrointestinal tract and then establishes infections in normally sterile sites within the body. The likelihood that *L. monocytogenes* can establish a systemic infection is dependent on a number of factors, including the number of micro-organisms consumed, host susceptibility, and virulence of the specific isolate ingested. Almost all strains of *L. monocytogenes* appear to be pathogenic, although their virulence, as defined in animal studies, varies substantially. Listeriosis is an infection that most often affects individuals experiencing immunosuppression, including individuals with chronic disease (e.g. cancer, diabetes, malnutrition, AIDS), foetuses or neonates (assumed to be infected *in utero*), the elderly and individuals being treated with immunosuppressive drugs (e.g. transplant patients). The bacterium most often affects the pregnant uterus, the central nervous system or the bloodstream.

---

[1] FAO. 2000. *Joint FAO/WHO Expert Consultation on Risk Assessment of Microbiological Hazards in Foods.* Food and Nutrition Paper No. 71. Rome.

Manifestations of listeriosis include but are not limited to bacteremia, septicaemia, meningitis, encephalitis, miscarriage, neonatal disease, premature birth, and stillbirth. Incubation periods prior to individuals becoming symptomatic can be from a few days up to three months. *L. monocytogenes* can also cause mild febrile gastroenteritis in otherwise healthy individuals. The public health significance of this type of listeriosis appears to be much lower than that of invasive listeriosis.

Available epidemiological data show invasive listeriosis occurs both as sporadic cases and outbreaks, with the former accounting for the majority of cases. Invasive listeriosis is a relatively rare, but often severe disease, with incidences typically of 3–8 cases per 1 000 000 individuals and fatality rates of 20–30 percent among hospitalized patients.[2] During recent years, the incidence of listeriosis in most countries has remained constant, with a number of countries reporting declines in the incidence of disease. These reductions probably reflect the efforts in those countries by industry and governments (a) to implement good hygienic practice (GHP) and apply Hazard Analysis and Critical Control Points (HACCP) to reduce the frequency and extent of *L. monocytogenes* in ready-to-eat foods, (b) to improve the integrity of the cold chain through processing, distribution, retail and the home to reduce the incidence of temperature abuse conditions that foster the growth of *L. monocytogenes*, and (c) to enhance risk communication, particularly for consumers at increased risk of listeriosis. However, further actions are needed to achieve continuous improvement of public health by lowering the incidence of human foodborne listeriosis worldwide. Periodically, transitory increases in incidence have been noted in several countries. These have been associated typically with foodborne outbreaks attributable to specific foods, often from specific manufacturers. In such cases, the incidence of listeriosis returned to prior baseline values after the causative food was removed from the market, and consumers received effective public health information pertaining to appropriate food choices and handling practices.

Listeriosis has been recognized as a human disease since the 1930s. However, it was not until the 1980s, when there were several large outbreaks in North America and Europe, that the role that foods play in the transmission of the disease was fully recognized. Foods are now considered to be the major vehicle for *L. monocytogenes*. A variety of specific foods have been implicated in outbreaks and sporadic cases of listeriosis (e.g. processed meats, soft cheeses, smoked fish, butter, milk, coleslaw). The foods associated with listeriosis have been overwhelmingly ready-to-eat products that are typically held for extended periods at refrigeration or chill temperatures.

The large number of ready-to-eat foods in which *L. monocytogenes* is at least occasionally isolated has made it difficult to effectively focus food control programmes on those specific foods that contribute the greatest risk to foodborne listeriosis. As a means of addressing this and a number of related questions, several formal quantitative

---

[2]   FAO and WHO. 2001. *Joint FAO/WHO Expert Consultation on Risk Assessment of Microbiological Hazards in Foods: Risk characterisation of* Salmonella *spp. in eggs and broiler chickens and* L. monocytogenes *in ready-to-eat foods.* Food and Nutrition Paper No. 72. Rome.

risk assessments have been undertaken to address issues related to the relative risks among different ready-to-eat foods and the factors that contribute to those risks. Available governmental risk assessments currently include (1) a comparative risk assessment of 23 categories of ready-to-eat foods conducted by the United States Food and Drug Administration (FDA) and the Food Safety and Inspection Service (FSIS),[3] (2) a comparative risk assessment of four ready-to-eat foods conducted by FAO/WHO JEMRA at the request of the Codex Committee on Food Hygiene,[4] and (3) a product/process pathway analysis conducted by the United States FSIS for processed meats,[5] which examined the risk of product contamination from food contact surfaces.

Each of these assessments articulates concepts that countries can use to identify and categorize those ready-to-eat products that represent a significant risk of foodborne listeriosis. Five key factors were identified as contributing strongly to the risk of listeriosis associated with ready-to-eat foods:
- amount and frequency of consumption of a food;
- frequency and extent of contamination of a food with *L. monocytogenes*;
- ability of the food to support the growth of *L. monocytogenes*;
- temperature of refrigerated/chilled food storage;
- duration of refrigerated/chilled storage.

A combination of interventions is generally more effective in controlling the risk rather than any single intervention (FDA/FSIS, 2003).[3]

In addition to the factors above, which influence the number of *L. monocytogenes* present in the food at the time of consumption, the susceptibility of an individual is important in determining the likelihood of listeriosis.

The risk assessments that have been conducted have consistently identified the impact that the ability of a food to support the growth of *L. monocytogenes* has on the risk of listeriosis. Those foods that are able to support growth during the normal shelf-life of a product increase substantially the risk that the food will contribute to foodborne listeriosis. Control of growth can be achieved by several different approaches, including reformulation of the product such that one or more of the parameters influencing the growth of the bacterium (e.g. pH, water activity, presence of inhibitory compounds) is altered so the food no longer supports growth. Alternatively, strict control of temperature so that ready-to-eat foods never exceed 6 °C (preferably 2–4 °C) and/or shortening the duration of the product refrigerated/chilled shelf-life are other means for ensuring that growth to any significant degree does not occur before the product is consumed.

[3] FDA/FSIS. 2003. *Quantitative assessment of the relative risk to public health from foodborne* Listeria monocytogenes *among selected categories of ready-to-eat foods* (available at www.cfsan.fda.gov).
[4] FAO/WHO. 2004. *Risk assessment of* Listeria monocytogenes *in ready-to-eat foods*. Technical Report. Microbiological Risk Assessment Series No. 5. Rome.
[5] FSIS Rule Designed to Reduce Listeria monocytogenes in Ready-to-Eat Meat and Poultry (available at http://www.fsis.usda.gov/factsheets/fsis_rule_designed_to_reduce_listeria/index.asp).

Many of the ready-to-eat products that are associated with foodborne listeriosis include a step in their production that is listericidal. Thus, the frequency and level of contamination of these products with *L. monocytogenes* is typically associated with the recontamination of the product prior to final packaging or from subsequent handling during marketing or home use. Thus, another strategy to control foodborne listeriosis is to reduce recontamination of the product and/or to introduce an additional mitigation treatment after final packaging. Control of the frequency and level of contamination is likely to be influenced strongly by factors such as attention to the design and maintenance of equipment and the integrity of the cold chain, the latter clearly being identified as a risk factor (i.e. the temperature of refrigerated/chilled storage).

Some ready-to-eat foods do not include a listericidal treatment. Product safety in those instances is dependent on steps taken during primary production, processing and subsequent distribution and use to minimize or reduce contamination/recontamination and to limit growth through maintaining the cold chain and limiting the duration of refrigerated storage.

The FAO/WHO risk assessment also clearly indicated that in order for food control programmes to be effective, they must be capable of consistently achieving the degree of control required; the risk of listeriosis is largely associated with failures to meet current standards for *L. monocytogenes*, be they at 0.04 or 100 CFU/g. The analyses conducted within that risk assessment clearly indicate that the greatest risk associated with ready-to-eat products is the small portion of the products with high contamination levels of *L. monocytogenes*. Thus, a key component of a successful risk management programme is assurance that control measures (e.g. preventing contamination and growth of the pathogen) can be achieved consistently.

SECTION 1 – OBJECTIVES

These Guidelines provide advice to governments on a framework for the control of *L. monocytogenes* in ready-to-eat foods, with a view towards protecting the health of consumers and ensuring fair practices in food trade. Their primary purpose is to minimize the likelihood of illness arising from the presence of *L. monocytogenes* in ready-to-eat foods. The Guidelines also provide information that will be of interest to the food industry, consumers and other interested parties.

SECTION 2 – SCOPE

2.1   Scope
These Guidelines are intended for ready-to-eat foods and are applicable throughout the food chain, from primary production through to consumption. However, based on the results of the FAO/WHO risk assessment, other available risk assessments and epidemiological evaluations, these Guidelines will focus on control measures that can be used, where appropriate, to minimize and/or prevent the contamination and/or the growth of *L. monocytogenes* in ready-to-eat foods. These Guidelines highlight key control measures that affect key factors that influence the frequency and extent

of contamination of ready-to-eat foods with *L. monocytogenes* and thus the risk of listeriosis. In many instances, these control measures are articulated in a general manner in the *Recommended International Code of Practice – General Principles of food hygiene* (CAC/RCP 1-1969) as part of the general strategy for control of foodborne pathogens in all foods. In providing these Guidelines, it is assumed that these general principles of food hygiene are being implemented. Those principles that are restated reflect the need for special attention for the control of *L. monocytogenes*.

Good hygienic practices (GHPs) as specified in the *Recommended International Code of Practice – General Principles of food hygiene* (CAC/RCP 1-1969) and other applicable codes of hygienic practice should be suitable to control *L. monocytogenes* in non ready-to-eat foods. However, the additional measures described in the following Guidelines should be consulted and implemented, as necessary, to control *L. monocytogenes* in ready-to-eat foods.

2.2 Definitions

For the purpose of these Guidelines, the following definitions apply:

Definitions of the *Principles and Guidelines for the conduct of microbiological risk management (MRM)* (CAC/GL 63-2007) apply.

Ready-to-eat food Any food that is normally eaten in its raw state or any food handled, processed, mixed, cooked, or otherwise prepared into a form that is normally eaten without further listericidal steps.

SECTION 3 – PRIMARY PRODUCTION

Many ready-to-eat foods receive one or more treatments during processing or preparation that inactivate or inhibit the growth of *L. monocytogenes*. For these foods, animal health and general application of good agricultural practices, including animal husbandry, should be sufficient to minimize the prevalence of *L. monocytogenes* at primary production.

In those ready-to-eat foods that are manufactured without a listericidal treatment, extra attention at primary production is needed to ensure specific control of the pathogen (e.g. control of *L. monocytogenes* mastitis in dairy cattle and sheep where the milk will be used to make raw milk cheeses, frequency of *L. monocytogenes* in raw milk as related to the feeding of inadequately fermented silage, high levels of *L. monocytogenes* in pork for fermented sausages resulting from wet feeding systems, faecal contamination of fresh produce), including increased focus on personal hygiene and water management programmes at the primary production sites.

Analysis of raw material for *L. monocytogenes* can be, where appropriate, an important tool for validating and verifying that the control measures at the primary production level are adequately limiting the frequency and level of contamination to that needed to achieve the required level of control during subsequent manufacturing.

3.1   Environmental hygiene
        Refer to the *Recommended International Code of Practice – General Principles of food hygiene* (CAC/RCP 1-1969).

3.2   Hygienic production of food sources
        Refer to the *Recommended International Code of Practice – General Principles of food hygiene* (CAC/RCP 1-1969).

3.3   Handling, storage and transport
        Refer to the *Recommended International Code of Practice – General Principles of food hygiene* (CAC/RCP 1-1969).

3.4.   Cleaning, maintenance and personnel hygiene at primary production
        Refer to the *Recommended International Code of Practice – General Principles of food hygiene* (CAC/RCP 1-1969).

SECTION 4 – ESTABLISHMENT: DESIGN AND FACILITIES

> **OBJECTIVES:**
> Equipment and facilities should be designed, constructed and laid out to ensure cleanability and to minimize the potential for *L. monocytogenes* harbourage sites, cross-contamination and recontamination.
> **RATIONALE:**
> - The introduction of *L. monocytogenes* into the ready-to-eat processing environment has resulted from inadequate separation of raw and finished product areas and from poor control of employees or equipment traffic.
> - Inability to clean and disinfect equipment and premises properly owing to poor layout or design and areas inaccessible to cleaning has resulted in biofilms containing *L. monocytogenes* and harbourage sites that have been a source of product contamination.
> - The use of spray cleaning procedures that aerosolize the micro-organism has been linked to the spread of the *L. monocytogenes* in the processing environment.
> - Inability to control ventilation properly to minimize condensate formation on surfaces in food-processing plants may result in the occurrence of *L. monocytogenes* in droplets and aerosols that can lead to product contamination.

4.1   Location

4.1.1   **Establishments**
        Refer to the *Recommended International Code of Practice – General Principles of food hygiene* (CAC/RCP 1-1969).

97

4.1.2   **Equipment**
Whenever possible, equipment should be designed and placed in a manner that facilitates access for efficient cleaning and disinfection, and thus avoid the formation of biofilms containing *L. monocytogenes* and harbourage sites.

4.2   Premises and rooms

4.2.1   **Design and layout**
Whenever feasible, premises and rooms should be designed to separate raw and finished ready-to-eat product areas. This can be accomplished in a number of ways, including linear product flow (raw to finished) with filtered airflow in the opposite direction (finished to raw) or physical partitions. Positive air pressure should be maintained on the finished side of the operation relative to the "raw" side (e.g. maintain lower air pressures in raw areas and higher pressures in finished areas).

Where feasible, the washing areas for food equipment involved in the manufacture of the finished product should be located in a separate room from the finished product processing area. This latter area should be separate from the raw ingredient handling area and the cleaning area for equipment used in the handling of raw ingredients in order to prevent recontamination of equipment and utensils used for finished products. Rooms where ready-to-eat products are exposed to the environment should be designed so that they can be maintained as dry as possible; wet operations often enhance the growth and spread of *L. monocytogenes*.

4.2.2   **New construction/renovations**
Owing to the ability of *L. monocytogenes* to survive in the plant environment for long periods of time, disturbances caused by construction or modification of layouts can cause reintroduction of *L. monocytogenes* from harbourage sites to the environment. Where appropriate, care should be taken to isolate the construction area, to enhance hygienic operations and to increase environmental monitoring to detect *Listeria* spp. during construction/renovation (see Section 6.5).

4.2.3   **Temporary/mobile premises and vending machines**
Refer to the *Recommended International Code of Practice – General Principles of food hygiene* (CAC/RCP 1-1969).

4.3   Equipment

4.3.1   **General**
Owing to the ability of *L. monocytogenes* to exist in biofilms and persist in harbourage sites for extended periods, processing equipment should be designed, constructed and maintained to avoid, for example, cracks, crevices, rough welds, hollow tubes and supports, close-fitting metal-to-metal or metal-to-plastic surfaces, worn seals and gaskets or other areas that cannot be reached during normal cleaning and disinfection of food contact surfaces and adjacent areas.

Racks or other equipment used for transporting exposed product should have easily cleaned cover guards over the wheels to prevent contamination of the food from wheel spray.

Cold surfaces (e.g. refrigeration units) can be sources for psychrotrophic bacteria, especially *L. monocytogenes*. Condensate from refrigeration unit pans should be directed to a drain via a hose or drip pans should be emptied, cleaned and disinfected on a regular basis.

Insulation should be designed and installed in such a manner that it does not become a harbourage site for *L. monocytogenes*.

4.3.2 **Food control and monitoring equipment**
Refer to the *Recommended International Code of Practice – General Principles of food hygiene* (CAC/RCP 1-1969).

4.3.3 **Containers for waste and inedible substances**
Refer to the *Recommended International Code of Practice – General Principles of food hygiene* (CAC/RCP 1-1969).

4.4 Facilities

4.4.1 **Water supply**
Refer to the *Recommended International Code of Practice – General Principles of food hygiene* (CAC/RCP 1-1969).

4.4.2 **Drainage and waste disposal**
Refer to the *Recommended International Code of Practice – General Principles of food hygiene* (CAC/RCP 1-1969).

4.4.3 **Cleaning**
Refer to the *Recommended International Code of Practice – General Principles of food hygiene* (CAC/RCP 1-1969).

4.4.4 **Personnel hygiene facilities and toilets**
Refer to the *Recommended International Code of Practice – General Principles of food hygiene* (CAC/RCP 1-1969).

4.4.5 **Temperature control**
Refer to the *Recommended International Code of Practice – General Principles of food hygiene* (CAC/RCP 1-1969).

4.4.6 **Air quality and ventilation**
Control of ventilation to minimize condensate formation is of particular importance in *L. monocytogenes* control, as the organism has been isolated from a wide variety of

surfaces in food-processing plants. Wherever feasible, facilities should be designed so that droplets and aerosols from condensates do not contaminate directly or indirectly food and food contact surfaces.

4.4.7	**Lighting**

Refer to the *Recommended International Code of Practice – General Principles of food hygiene* (CAC/RCP 1-1969).

4.4.8	**Storage**

Where feasible and appropriate for the food product, and where food ingredients and products support growth of *L. monocytogenes*, storage rooms should be designed so that a product temperature should not exceed 6 °C, (preferably 2–4 °C). Raw materials should be stored separately from finished, processed products.

SECTION 5 – CONTROL OF OPERATION

OBJECTIVES:
Processing operations should be controlled to reduce the frequency and level of contamination in the finished product, to minimize the growth of *L. monocytogenes* in the finished product and to reduce the likelihood that the product will be recontaminated and/or will support the growth of *L. monocytogenes* during subsequent distribution, marketing and home use.
RATIONALE:
For many ready-to-eat products, listericidal processes[6] can ensure appropriate reduction in risk. However, not all ready-to-eat products receive such a treatment and other ready-to-eat products may be exposed to the environment and thus may be subject to potential recontamination. Prevention of cross-contamination, strict control of time and temperature for products in which *L. monocytogenes* can grow and formulation of products with hurdles to *L. monocytogenes* growth can minimize the risk of listeriosis.

5.1	Control of the food hazard

Control of *L. monocytogenes* for many ready-to-eat products will typically require a stringent application of GHPs and other supportive programmes. These prerequisite programmes, together with HACCP, provide a successful framework for the control of *L. monocytogenes*.

The factors and attributes described below are components of GHP programmes that will typically require elevated attention to control *L. monocytogenes* and may be identified as critical control points in HACCP programmes where *L. monocytogenes* is identified as a hazard.

---

[6] Any appropriate treatment that kills *Listeria*.

5.2 Key aspects of hygiene control systems

5.2.1 Time and temperature control

The risk assessments done by the United States FDA/FSIS and FAO/WHO on *L. monocytogenes* in ready-to-eat foods demonstrated the tremendous influence of storage temperature on the risk of listeriosis associated with ready-to-eat foods that support *L. monocytogenes* growth. It is therefore necessary to control the time/temperature combination used for storage.

Monitoring and controlling refrigerated storage temperatures are key control measures. The product temperature should not exceed 6 °C (preferably 2–4 °C). Temperature abuse that may occur supporting the growth of *L. monocytogenes* could result in a reduction of product shelf-life.

The length of the shelf-life is another important factor contributing to the risk associated with foods that support *L. monocytogenes* growth. The shelf-life of such foods should be consistent with the need to control the growth of *L. monocytogenes*. As *L. monocytogenes* is able to grow under refrigeration temperatures, the length of the shelf-life should be based on appropriate studies that assess the growth of *L. monocytogenes* in the food. Shelf-life studies and other information are important tools facilitating the selection of the length of shelf-life. If they are conducted, they should account for the fact that appropriate low temperatures may not be maintained throughout the entire food chain until the point of consumption. Temperature abuses may allow the growth of *L. monocytogenes*, if present, unless appropriate intrinsic factors are applied to prevent such growth. This should be taken into account when establishing shelf-life.

5.2.2 Specific process steps

Listericidal processes should be validated to ensure that the treatments are effective and can be applied consistently (see Section V of the *Recommended International Code of Practice – General Principles of food hygiene* [CAC/RCP 1-1969]).

In some products, single parameters, such as a pH less than 4.4, a water activity less than 0.92 or freezing, may be relied upon to prevent *L. monocytogenes* growth. In other products, a combination of parameters is used. Validation should be undertaken to ensure the effectiveness of these parameters in situations where combinations of parameters or bacteriostatic conditions are relied upon.

Products supporting the growth of *L. monocytogenes* that have undergone a listericidal treatment may be contaminated/recontaminated before final packaging. In these cases, additional control measures may be applied if necessary (e.g. freezing the product, shortening the shelf-life, reformulation of the product) to limit the extent of or prevent *L. monocytogenes* growth. Alternatively, a post-packaging listericidal treatment may be necessary (e.g. heating, high-pressure treatment, irradiation, where accepted).

In raw, ready-to-eat foods (e.g. lettuce) that support the growth of *L. monocytogenes* and that may be contaminated, specific control measures may be applied if necessary to limit the extent of or prevent the growth of *L. monocytogenes* (e.g. acid wash).

5.2.3	**Microbiological and other specifications**

Refer to the *Recommended International Code of Practice – General Principles of food hygiene* (CAC/RCP 1-1969) and *Principles for the establishment and application of microbiological criteria for foods* (CAC/GL 21-1979).

5.2.4	**Microbiological cross-contamination**

Microbiological cross-contamination is a major issue with respect to *L. monocytogenes*. It can occur through direct contact with raw materials, personnel, aerosols and contaminated utensils, equipment, etc. Cross-contamination can occur at any step where the product is exposed to the environment, including processing, transportation, retail, catering, and in the home.

Traffic flow patterns for employees, food products and equipment should be controlled between raw processing, storage area(s) and finished area(s) to minimize the transfer of *L. monocytogenes*. For example, a change of footwear or automated foam sprayers can be an effective alternative to footbaths where people, carts, forklifts and other portable equipment must enter an area where ready-to-eat foods are exposed. Another example is to use a colour coding system to identify personnel assigned to specific areas of the plant.

Utensils, pallets, carts, forklifts and mobile racks should be dedicated for use in either the raw area or the finished product area to minimize cross-contamination. Where this is not practical, they should be cleaned and disinfected before entry into the finished product area.

Reused brines and recycled process water used in direct contact with finished product should be discarded or decontaminated (e.g. chlorination for recycled water, heat treatment, or some other effective treatment) with sufficient frequency to ensure control of *L. monocytogenes*.

Ready-to eat foods that do not support the growth of *L. monocytogenes* but may have low levels of this pathogen should not be a source of contamination to other ready-to-eat foods that may support the growth of this pathogen. Consideration should be given to the fact that some ready-to-eat foods with special handling requirements (e.g. ice cream) that are handled after opening may present a lower risk for being a vector for cross contaminating other ready-to-eat foods, because such specially handled product is rapidly consumed. Other ready-to-eat products, however, with special formulation (e.g. dry fermented sausage), that are handled after opening may present a higher risk of being a vector for cross contaminating other ready-to-eat products if neither ready-to-eat product is rapidly consumed.

5.2.5 **Physical and chemical contamination**

Refer to the *Recommended International Code of Practice – General Principles of food hygiene* (CAC/RCP 1-1969).

5.3 Incoming material requirements

Refer to the *Recommended International Code of Practice – General Principles of food hygiene* (CAC/RCP 1-1969).

5.4 Packaging

Refer to the *Recommended International Code of Practice – General Principles of food hygiene* (CAC/RCP 1-1969).

5.5 Water

Refer to the *Recommended International Code of Practice – General Principles of food hygiene* (CAC/RCP 1-1969).

5.5.1 **In contact with food**

Refer to the *Recommended International Code of Practice – General Principles of food hygiene* (CAC/RCP 1-1969).

5.5.2 **As an ingredient**

Refer to the *Recommended International Code of Practice – General Principles of food hygiene* (CAC/RCP 1-1969).

5.5.3 **Ice and steam**

Refer to the *Recommended International Code of Practice – General Principles of food hygiene* (CAC/RCP 1-1969).

5.6 Management and supervision

Refer to the *Recommended International Code of Practice – General Principles of food hygiene* (CAC/RCP 1-1969).

5.7 Documentation and records

Refer to the *Recommended International Code of Practice – General Principles of food hygiene* (CAC/RCP 1-1969).

5.8 Recall procedures

Based on the determined level of risk associated with the presence of *L. monocytogenes* in a given food product, a decision may be taken to recall the contaminated product from the market. In some instances, the need for public warnings should be considered.

5.9 Monitoring of effectiveness of control measures for *L. monocytogenes*

An effective environmental monitoring programme is an essential component of a *Listeria* control programme, particularly in establishments that produce ready-to-eat foods that support growth and may contain *L. monocytogenes*. Testing of food products can be another component of verification that control measures for *L. monocytogenes* are effective (see Section 5.2.3).

Recommendations for the design of an environmental monitoring programme for *L. monocytogenes* in processing areas are given in Annex 1.

SECTION 6 – ESTABLISHMENT: MAINTENANCE AND SANITATION

OBJECTIVES:
To provide specific guidance on how preventive maintenance and sanitation procedures, along with an effective environmental monitoring programme can reduce contamination of food with *L. monocytogenes*, particularly when the foods support growth of *L. monocytogenes*:

Well-structured cleaning and disinfection procedures should be targeted against *L. monocytogenes* in food-processing areas where ready-to-eat foods are exposed to reduce:
- the likelihood that the product will be contaminated after processing;
- the level of contamination in the finished product.

RATIONALE:
Basic cleaning and disinfection programmes are critical to ensuring control of *L. monocytogenes.* An environmental monitoring programme for *Listeria* in processing areas where ready-to-eat foods are exposed is necessary to assess the effectiveness of control measures and, therefore, the likelihood of contamination of the food.

6.1 Maintenance and cleaning

6.1.1 General

Establishments should implement an effective, scheduled preventive maintenance programme to prevent equipment failures during operation and the development of harbourage sites. Equipment failures during production increase the risk of *L. monocytogenes* contamination as equipment is being repaired. The preventive maintenance programme should be written and include a defined maintenance schedule.

The preventive maintenance programme should include scheduled replacement or repair of equipment before it becomes a source of contamination. Equipment should be inspected periodically for parts that are cracked, worn or have developed spaces where food and moisture accumulate (i.e. harbourage sites). Preventive maintenance should include periodic examination and maintenance of conveyors, filters, gaskets, pumps, slicers, filling equipment, and packaging machines and support structures for equipment. Air filters for bringing outside air into the plant should be examined and changed based on manufacturer's specification or more frequently based on pressure differential or microbiological monitoring.

Wherever possible, tools used for maintenance of equipment to which ready-to-eat foods are exposed should be dedicated to the finished product area. Such tools should be washed and disinfected prior to use. Maintenance personnel in the finished product area should comply with the same hygiene requirements as the finished product production employees. Food contact surfaces on equipment should be cleaned and disinfected after maintenance work, prior to production use. Equipment that could have become contaminated during maintenance work on facility utilities, e.g. air system, water system, etc., or remodelling should be cleaned and disinfected prior to use.

6.1.2 Cleaning procedures and methods

Experience indicates that over-reliance on chemicals alone for cleaning can lead to increased levels of microbial contamination. The chemicals must be applied at the recommended use-concentration, for sufficient time, at the recommended temperature and with sufficient force (i.e. turbulence, scrubbing) to remove soil and biofilm. Instances of *L. monocytogenes* contamination have been linked, in particular, to insufficient manual scrubbing during the cleaning process.

Research and experience further indicate that *L. monocytogenes* does not possess an unusual ability to resist disinfectants or attach to surfaces. However, it is noted that *L. monocytogenes* has the ability to form biofilms on a variety of surfaces.

Solid forms of disinfectants (e.g. blocks of quaternary ammonium compounds [QACs]) can be placed in the drip pan of refrigeration units and solid rings containing disinfectants can be placed in drains to help control *L. monocytogenes* in drains. Granulated forms of disinfectants such as QACs, hydrogen peroxide and peroxyacetic acid can be applied to floors after routine cleaning and disinfecting. The development of antimicrobial resistance should be considered in the application and use of disinfectants.

The equipment used for cleaning, e.g. brushes, bottle brushes, mops, floor scrubbers, and vacuum cleaners, should be maintained and cleaned so they do not become a source of contamination. The cleaning equipment should be dedicated for either raw areas or finished areas, and easily distinguishable (e.g. colour-coded cleaning tools).

To prevent aerosols from contacting ready-to-eat foods, food contact surfaces and food packaging materials, high-pressure water hoses should not be used during production or after equipment has been cleaned and disinfected.

It has been shown that *L. monocytogenes* can become established and persist in floor drains. Therefore, drains should be cleaned and disinfected in a manner that prevents contamination of other surfaces in the room. Utensils for cleaning drains should be easily distinguishable and be dedicated to that purpose to minimize the potential for contamination.

Floor drains should not be cleaned during production. High-pressure hoses should not be used to clear or clean a drain, as aerosols will be created that spread contamination throughout the room. If a drain backup occurs in finished product areas, production should stop until the water has been removed and the areas have been cleaned and disinfected. Employees who have been cleaning drains should not contact or clean food contact surfaces without changing clothes, and washing and disinfecting hands.

6.2   Cleaning programmes
The effectiveness of sanitation programmes should be periodically verified and the programmes modified as necessary to ensure the consistent achievement of the level of control needed for a food operation to prevent *L. monocytogenes* contamination of ready-to-eat food and ready-to-eat food contact surfaces.

6.3   Pest control systems
Refer to the *Recommended International Code of Practice – General Principles of food hygiene* (CAC/RCP 1-1969).

6.3.1   **General**
Refer to the *Recommended International Code of Practice – General Principles of food hygiene* (CAC/RCP 1-1969).

6.3.2   **Preventing access**
Refer to the *Recommended International Code of Practice – General Principles of food hygiene* (CAC/RCP 1-1969).

6.3.3   **Harbourage and infestation**
Refer to the *Recommended International Code of Practice – General Principles of food hygiene* (CAC/RCP 1-1969).

6.3.4   **Monitoring and detection**
Refer to the *Recommended International Code of Practice – General Principles of food hygiene* (CAC/RCP 1-1969).

6.3.5   **Eradication**
Refer to the *Recommended International Code of Practice – General Principles of food hygiene* (CAC/RCP 1-1969).

6.4   Waste management
Refer to the *Recommended International Code of Practice – General Principles of food hygiene* (CAC/RCP 1-1969).

6.5   **Monitoring effectiveness**

Environmental monitoring (see Section 5.9) can also be used to verify the effectiveness of sanitation programmes such that sources of contamination of *L. monocytogenes* are identified and corrected in a timely manner. Recommendations for the design of an environmental monitoring programme in processing areas are given in Annex 1.

SECTION 7 – ESTABLISHMENT: PERSONAL HYGIENE

> **OBJECTIVES:**
> To prevent workers from transferring *L. monocytogenes* from contaminated surfaces to food or food contact surfaces.
> **RATIONALE:**
> Workers can serve as a vehicle for cross-contamination and should be aware of the steps that need to be taken to manage this risk.

7.1   **Health status**

Refer to the *Recommended International Code of Practice – General Principles of food hygiene* (CAC/RCP 1-1969).

7.2   **Illness and injuries**

Refer to the *Recommended International Code of Practice – General Principles of food hygiene* (CAC/RCP 1-1969).

7.3   **Personal cleanliness**

Refer to the *Recommended International Code of Practice – General Principles of food hygiene* (CAC/RCP 1-1969).

7.4   **Personal behaviour**

Employee hygienic practices play an important role in preventing contamination of exposed ready-to-eat foods with *L. monocytogenes*. For example, employees who handle trash, floor sweepings, drains, packaging waste or scrap product, should not touch the food, touch food contact surfaces or food packaging material, unless they change their smock or outer clothing, wash and disinfect hands, and wear clean new gloves for tasks requiring gloves. Adequate training and supervision should be provided to ensure hygienic practices are accomplished.

7.5   **Visitors**

Refer to the *Recommended International Code of Practice – General Principles of food hygiene* (CAC/RCP 1-1969).

SECTION 8 – TRANSPORTATION

> **OBJECTIVES:**
> Measures should be taken where necessary to:
> - protect food from potential sources of contamination including harbourage sites for *L. monocytogenes* in transportation equipment and to prevent the co-mingling of raw and ready-to-eat product;
> - provide an adequately refrigerated environment (so that product temperature should not exceed 6 °C, preferably 2–4 °C).
>
> **RATIONALE:**
> Food may become contaminated during transportation if not properly protected.
> If refrigeration is inadequate, food may support the growth of *L. monocytogenes* to higher levels.

8.1 **General**

Transportation is an integral step in the food chain and should be controlled, particularly the product temperature, which should not exceed 6 °C (preferably 2–4 °C).

Transportation vehicles should be regularly inspected for structural integrity, cleanliness and overall suitability when unloading ingredients and prior to loading finished products. In particular, the structural integrity of transportation vehicles (e.g. tanker trucks) should be monitored for stress cracks that act as harbourage sites for *L. monocytogenes*. Tankers should be dedicated to transporting either ingredients or finished products.

8.2 **Requirements**

Refer to the *Recommended International Code of Practice – General Principles of food hygiene* (CAC/RCP 1-1969).

8.3 **Use and maintenance**

Food transportation units, accessories and connections should be cleaned, disinfected (where appropriate) and maintained to avoid or at least reduce the risk of contamination. It should be noted that different commodities may require different cleaning procedures. Where necessary, disinfection should be followed by rinsing unless manufacturer's instructions indicate on a scientific basis that rinsing is not required.[7] A record should be available that indicates when cleaning occurred.

---

[7] *Code of hygienic practice for the transport of food in bulk and semi-packed food* (CAC/RCP 47-2001).

SECTION 9 – PRODUCT INFORMATION AND CONSUMER AWARENESS

OBJECTIVES:
Consumers should have enough knowledge of *L. monocytogenes* and food hygiene such that they:
- understand the importance of shelf-life, sell-by or use-by dates written on food label;
- can make informed choices appropriate to the individual's health status and concomitant risk of acquiring foodborne listeriosis;
- prevent contamination and growth or survival of *L. monocytogenes* by adequately storing and preparing ready-to-eat foods.

Health care providers should have appropriate information on *L. monocytogenes* in foods and listeriosis to give advice to consumers and in particular susceptible populations.

RATIONALE:
Consumers (in particular, the susceptible populations) and health care providers need to be informed about ready-to-eat foods supporting growth of *L. monocytogenes,* food handling, preparation practices and avoidance of certain foods by susceptible populations.

9.1 Lot identification
Refer to the *Recommended International Code of Practice – General Principles of food hygiene* (CAC/RCP 1-1969).

9.2 Product information
Refer to the *Recommended International Code of Practice – General Principles of food hygiene* (CAC/RCP 1-1969).

9.3 Labelling
Countries should give consideration to labelling of certain ready-to-eat foods so that consumers can make an informed choice with regard to these products. Where appropriate, product labels should include information on safe handling practices and/ or advice on the time frames in which the product should be eaten.

9.4 Consumer education
As each country has specific consumption habits, communication programmes pertaining to *L. monocytogenes* are most effective when established by individual governments.

Programmes for consumer information should be directed:
- at consumers with increased susceptibility to contracting listeriosis, such as pregnant women, the elderly and immunocompromised persons;

109

- to help consumers make informed choices about purchase, storage, shelf-life labelling and appropriate consumption of certain ready-to-eat foods that have been identified in relevant risk assessment and other studies, taking into consideration the specific regional conditions and consumption habits;
- to consumers to educate them on household practices and behaviours that would specifically keep the numbers of *L. monocytogenes* that may be present in foods, to as low a level as possible by:
  - setting refrigerator temperatures so that product temperatures should not exceed 6 °C (preferably 2–4 °C) as the growth of *L. monocytogenes* is considerably reduced at temperatures below 6 °C;
  - frequently washing and disinfecting the household refrigerator as *L. monocytogenes* can be present in many foods and grow at refrigerator temperatures, and thus contribute to cross-contamination;
  - respecting the shelf-life dates written on ready-to-eat foods;
  - using thermometers inside home refrigerators.

Programmes for health care providers should, in addition to information provided to consumers, be designed to provide them with guidance that:
- facilitates rapid diagnosis of foodborne listeriosis;
- provides means to communicate rapidly information on preventing listeriosis to their patients, particularly those with increased susceptibility.

SECTION 10 – TRAINING

OBJECTIVE:
Those engaged in food operation who come directly or indirectly in contact with ready-to-eat foods should be trained and/or instructed in the control of *L. monocytogenes* to a level appropriate to the operations they are to perform.
RATIONALE:
Controls specific to *L. monocytogenes* are generally more stringent than routine GHPs.

10.1   Awareness and responsibilities
Industry (primary producers, manufacturers, distributors, retailers and food service/ institutional establishments) and trade associations have an important role in providing specific instruction and training for control of *L. monocytogenes*.

10.2   Training programmes
Personnel involved with the production and handling of ready-to-eat food should have appropriate training in:
- the nature of *L. monocytogenes*, its harbourage sites, and its resistance to various environmental conditions to be able to conduct a suitable hazard analysis for their products;

- control measures for reducing the risk of *L. monocytogenes* associated with ready-to-eat foods during processing, distribution, marketing, use and storage;
- the means for verifying effectiveness of control programmes, including sampling and analytical techniques;

10.3 Instruction and supervision

Refer to the *Recommended International Code of Practice – General Principles of food hygiene* (CAC/RCP 1-1969).

10.4 Refresher training

Refer to the *Recommended International Code of Practice – General Principles of food hygiene* (CAC/RCP 1-1969).

RECOMMENDATIONS FOR AN ENVIRONMENTAL MONITORING[8] PROGRAMME FOR *LISTERIA MONOCYTOGENES* IN PROCESSING AREAS

Manufacturers of ready-to-eat foods should consider the potential risk to consumers in the event their products contain *L. monocytogenes* when they are released for distribution. The necessity for an environmental monitoring programme is highest for ready-to-eat foods that support *L. monocytogenes* growth and that are not given a post-packaging listericidal treatment. Recontamination has led to many of the recognized outbreaks of listeriosis. One effective element for managing this risk is to implement a monitoring programme to assess control of the environment in which ready-to-eat foods are exposed prior to final packaging.

A number of factors (a – i) should be considered when developing the sampling programme to ensure the programme's effectiveness:

a) **Type of product and process/operation**
The need[9] for and extent of the sampling programme should be defined according to the characteristics of the ready-to-eat foods (supporting or not supporting growth), the type of processing (listericidal or not) and the likelihood of contamination or recontamination (exposed to the environment or not). In addition, consideration also needs to be given to elements such as the general hygiene status of the plant or the existing history of *L. monocytogenes* in the environment.

b) **Type of samples**
Environmental samples consist of both food contact and non-food contact surface samples. Food contact surfaces, in particular those after the listericidal step and prior to packaging, have a higher probability of directly contaminating the product, while for non-food contact surfaces the likelihood will depend on the location and practices.

Raw materials may serve as a source of environmental contamination and may therefore be included in the monitoring programme.

c) **Target organisms**
While this document addresses *L. monocytogenes*, effective monitoring programmes may also involve testing for *Listeria* spp; their presence is a good indicator of conditions

---

[8] Environmental monitoring is not to be confused with monitoring as defined in the Hazard Analysis and Critical Control Point (HACCP) system.
[9] Products such as in-pack pasteurized foods that are not further exposed to environment may not necessarily require a monitoring.

supporting the potential presence of *L. monocytogenes*. Where appropriate and shown to be valid, other indicator organisms may be used.[10]

d) **Sampling locations and number of samples**
The number of samples will vary with the complexity of the process and the food being produced.

Information on appropriate locations can be found in published literature, and can be based on process experience or expertise or in plant surveys. Sampling locations should be reviewed on a regular basis. Additional locations may need to be sampled depending on special situations such as major maintenance or construction or when new or modified equipment has been installed.

e) **Frequency of sampling**
The frequency of environmental sampling would be based primarily on the factors outlined under subheading "Type of product and process/operation". It should be defined according to existing data on the presence of *Listeria* spp. and/or *L. monocytogenes* in the environment of the operation under consideration.

In the absence of such information, sufficient suitable data should be generated to define correctly the appropriate frequency. These data should be collected over a sufficiently long period as to provide reliable information on the prevalence of *Listeria* spp. and/or *L. monocytogenes* and the variations over time.

The frequency of environmental sampling may need to be increased as a result of finding *Listeria* spp. and/or *L. monocytogenes* in environmental samples. This will depend on the significance of the findings (e.g. *L. monocytogenes* and a risk of direct contamination of the product).

f) **Sampling tools and techniques**
It is important to adapt the type of sampling tools and techniques to the type of surfaces and sampling locations. For example, sponges may be used for large flat surfaces, swabs may be more appropriate for cracks and crevices or scrapers for hard residues.

g) **Analytical methods**
The analytical methods used to analyse environmental samples should be suitable for the detection of *L. monocytogenes* and of other defined target organisms. Considering the characteristics of environmental samples, it is important to demonstrate that the methods are able to detect, with acceptable sensitivity, the target organisms. This should be documented appropriately.

---

[10] Attributes contributing to the scientific support of the use of an indicator organism in view of a specific pathogen include: similar survival and growth characteristics; a shared common source for both organisms; direct relationship between the state or condition that contributes to the presence of the pathogen and the indicator organism; and practical, isolation, detection or enumeration methods for the potential indicator organism.

Under certain circumstances, it may be possible to composite (pool) certain samples without losing the required sensitivity. However, in the case of positive findings, additional testing will be necessary to determine the location of the positive sample.

Fingerprinting isolates by one or more of the available genetic techniques (e.g. pulsed field gel electrophoresis, ribotyping) can provide very useful information about the source(s) of L. monocytogenes *and pathway(s) that lead to contamination of the food.*

h) **Data management**
The monitoring programme should include a system to record the data and their evaluation, e.g. performing trend analyses. A long-term review of the data is important to revise and adjust monitoring programmes. It can also reveal low-level, intermittent contamination that may otherwise go unnoticed.

i) **Actions in case of positive results**
The purpose of the monitoring programme is to find *L. monocytogenes* or other target organisms if present in the environment. Generally, manufacturers should expect to find them occasionally in the processing environment. Therefore, an appropriate action plan should be designed and established to respond adequately to positive findings. A review of hygiene procedures and controls should be considered.

The manufacturer should react to each positive result; the nature of the reaction will depend upon the likelihood of contaminating the product and the expected use of the products.

The plan should define the specific action to be taken and the rationale. This could range from no action (no risk of recontamination), to intensified cleaning, to source tracing (increased environmental testing), to review of hygienic practices up to holding and testing of product.

ANNEX 2

MICROBIOLOGICAL CRITERIA FOR *LISTERIA MONOCYTOGENES* IN READY-TO-EAT FOODS

1. **Introduction**

   The microbiological criteria presented in this Annex are intended as advice to governments within a framework for control of *L. monocytogenes* in ready-to-eat foods with a view towards protecting the health of consumers and ensuring fair practices in food trade. They also provide information that may be of interest to industry.

   This Annex references and takes into account the *Principles for the establishment and application of microbiological criteria for foods* (CAC/GL 21-1997) and uses definitions, e.g. for microbiological criterion, as included in these Principles. The provisions of this Annex should be used in conjunction with Annex 2 of "Guidance on microbiological risk management metrics" of the *Principles and Guidelines for the conduct of microbiological risk management (MRM)* (CAC/GL 63-2007).

   The risk assessments referenced in the introduction to the *Guidelines on the application of general principles of food hygiene to the control of* Listeria monocytogenes *in ready-to-eat food* (CAC/GL 61-2007) have indicated that food can be categorized according to the likelihood of *L. monocytogenes* being present and its ability to grow in the food. Available risk assessments have been taken into account in the development of the microbiological criteria in this Annex. In addition, factors that might affect the ability of governments to implement these microbiological criteria, such as methodological limitations, costs associated with different types of quantitative testing, and statistics-based sampling needs, have been taken into account.

2. **Scope**

   These microbiological criteria apply to specific categories of ready-to-eat foods as described herein. The competent authority should consider the intended use and how specific ready-to-eat foods are likely to be handled during marketing, catering or by consumers to determine the appropriateness of applying the microbiological criteria. Governments may apply these criteria, where appropriate, to assess the acceptability of ready-to-eat foods in international trade for imported products, at end of manufacture (finished product) for domestic products, and at point of sale for at least the expected shelf-life[11] under reasonably foreseeable conditions of distribution, storage and use.

   The microbiological criteria may be used as the basis for the development of additional criteria (e.g. process criteria, product criteria) within a food safety control system[12] to ensure compliance with these Guidelines.

---

[11] See definition in the *Code of hygienic practice for milk and milk products* (CAC/RCP 57-2004).
[12] See *Guidelines for the validation of food safety control measures* (CAC/GL 69-2008).

Different criteria or other limits may be applied when the competent authority determines that the use of such an approach provides an acceptable level of public health or when the competent authority determines a more stringent criterion is necessary to protect public health.

3.   **Use of microbiological criteria for *L. monocytogenes* in ready-to-eat foods**
There are various applications for microbiological criteria. As described, microbiological testing by lot can be used as a direct control measure, i.e. sorting of acceptable and unacceptable lots.[13] In this instance, microbiological criteria are implemented for those products and/or points of the food chain when other more effective tools are not available and where the microbiological criteria would be expected to improve the degree of protection offered to the consumer.

A microbiological criterion defines the acceptability of a product or food lot based on the absence or presence or number of micro-organisms in the product. Testing for compliance with a microbiological criterion may be conducted on a lot-by-lot basis when there is little information about the conditions under which the product has been produced. Where there is information about the conditions of production, testing of lots for verification purposes may be conducted less frequently.

In addition, the application of the Hazard Analysis and Critical Control Point (HACCP) system describes how microbiological testing against a criterion can be used as a means of verifying the continuing effectiveness of a food safety control system.[14] Typically, such applications involve testing on less than a lot-by-lot basis and may be formalized into a system of process control verification testing (see Annex III).

Where possible and practicable, the risk-based approach to development of microbiological criteria as described in the *Principles and Guidelines for the conduct of microbiological risk management (MRM)* (CAC/GL-63-2007) can be used to ensure, or contribute to the assurance, that a food control system will achieve the required level of consumer protection.

The competent authority should use a risk-based approach to sampling for *L. monocytogenes* such as that found in the General guidelines on sampling (CAC/GL 50-2004). It may consider modifying the frequency of testing for process control verification based on additional consideration of the likelihood of contamination, characteristics of the food, product history, conditions of production and other relevant information. For example, testing against microbiological criteria may have limited utility immediately following certain processing steps or if the level of *L. monocytogenes* in a ready-to-eat food is consistently well below the limit of detection taking into account practical limits for sample sizes.

---

[13] See *Principles for the establishment and application of microbiological criteria for foods* (CAC/GL 21-1997).
[14] See *Recommended International Code of Practice – General Principles of food hygiene* (CAC/RCP 1-1969).

In particular, testing against microbiological criteria for *L. monocytogenes* may not be useful for:

(a) products that receive a listericidal treatment after being sealed in final packaging that ensures prevention of recontamination until opened by the consumer or otherwise compromised;

(b) foods that are aseptically processed and packaged;[15] and

(c) products that contain a listericidal component that ensures rapid inactivation of the pathogen if recontaminated (e.g. products that contain > 5 percent ethanol).

Competent authorities may define other categories of products for which testing against microbiological criteria is not useful.

Different types of food present different risks from *L. monocytogenes*; hence, different microbiological criteria could apply for the following categories of foods:

(a) ready-to-eat foods in which growth of *L. monocytogenes* will not occur; and

(b) ready-to-eat foods in which growth of *L. monocytogenes* can occur.

3.1 Ready-to-eat foods in which growth of *L. monocytogenes* will not occur

Ready-to-eat foods in which growth of *L. monocytogenes* will not occur would be determined based on scientific justification,[16] including the inherent variability of factors controlling *L. monocytogenes* in the product. Factors such as pH, a_w, are useful in preventing growth. For example, *L. monocytogenes* growth can be controlled in foods that have:

- a pH below 4.4;
- an $a_w < 0.92$;
- a combination of factors (pH, a_w), e.g. the combination of pH < 5.0 with $a_w < 0.94$.

Such growth can also be controlled by freezing (during that period when the product remains frozen).

In addition, inhibitors can control the growth of *L. monocytogenes* and synergy may be obtained with other extrinsic and intrinsic factors that would result in no growth.

Demonstration that *L. monocytogenes* will not grow in a ready-to-eat food can be based upon, for example, food characteristics, the study of naturally contaminated food, challenge tests, predictive modelling, information from the scientific literature and risk assessments, historical records or combinations of these. Such studies would generally be conducted by food business operators (or by the appropriate product board, sector organizations or contract laboratories) and must be appropriately designed to validate that *L. monocytogenes* will not grow in a food.[17]

---

[15] See *Code of hygienic practice for aseptically processed and packaged low-acid foods* (CAC/RCP 40-1993).

[16] References that have been addressed for identifying properties of ready-to-eat foods that will categorize them as foods in which growth of *L. monocytogenes* will not occur, or as foods in which growth of the pathogen can occur, include *Microorganisms in foods 5 – characteristics of microbial pathogens* (ICMSF, 1996) and *Risk assessment of* Listeria monocytogenes *in ready-to-eat foods: interpretative summary and technical report* (FAO/WHO, 2004).

[17] See *Guidelines for the validation of food safety control measures* (CAC/GL 69-2008).

The demonstration that *L. monocytogenes* will not grow in a ready-to-eat food should take into account the measurement error of the quantification method. Therefore, for example, for practical purposes, a food in which growth of *L. monocytogenes* will not occur will not have an observable increase in *L. monocytogenes* levels greater than (on average) 0.5 log CFU/g[18] for at least the expected shelf-life as labelled by the manufacturer under reasonably foreseeable conditions of distribution, storage and use, including a safety margin.

For foods intended to be refrigerated, studies to assess whether or not growth of *L. monocytogenes* will occur should be conducted under reasonably foreseeable conditions of distribution, storage and use.

National governments should provide guidance on the specific protocols that should be employed to validate the studies demonstrating that growth of *L. monocytogenes* will not occur in a food during the expected shelf-life.

If information is lacking to demonstrate that *L. monocytogenes* will not grow in a ready-to-eat food during its expected shelf-life, the food should be treated as a ready-to-eat food in which growth of *L. monocytogenes* can occur.

3.2   **Ready-to-eat foods in which growth of *L. monocytogenes* can occur**
A ready-to-eat food in which there is greater than an average of 0.5 log CFU/g[18] increase in *L. monocytogenes* levels for at least the expected shelf-life under reasonably foreseeable conditions of distribution, storage and use is considered a food in which growth of *L. monocytogenes* can occur.

4.   Microbiological criteria for *L. monocytogenes* in ready-to-eat foods
Microbiological criteria for *L. monocytogenes* in ready-to-eat foods are described.

Another procedure for establishing microbiological criteria for *L. monocytogenes* other than the criteria at specified points in the food chain that are described below, would be through the application of risk-based metrics (e.g. food safety objective [FSO], performance objective [PO]) according to the general principles established in Annex 2 "Guidance on microbiological risk management metrics" of the *Principles and Guidelines for the conduct of microbiological risk management (MRM)* (CAC/GL 63-2007).

---

[18] 0.5 log is two times the estimated standard deviation (i.e. 0.25 log) associated with the experimental enumeration using viable counting/plate counts.

4.1 Microbiological criteria for ready-to-eat foods in which growth of *L. monocytogenes* will not occur

The criterion in Table 1 is intended for foods in which *L. monocytogenes* growth will not occur under the conditions of storage and use that have been established for the product (see Section 3.1).

This criterion is based on the product being produced under application of the provisions of the General Principles of food hygiene to the control of *L. monocytogenes* in ready-to-eat foods with appropriate evaluation of the production environment and process control and validation that the product meets the requirements of a food in which growth of *L. monocytogenes* will not occur (see Section 3.1).

If the factors that prevent growth cannot be demonstrated, the product should be evaluated based on criteria for ready-to-eat foods in which growth of *L. monocytogenes* can occur (see Section 4.2).

Another approach can also be used (see Section 4.3).

TABLE 1

Microbiological criterion for ready-to-eat foods in which growth of *L. monocytogenes* will not occur

Point of application	Micro-organism	n	c	m	Class plan
Ready-to-eat foods from the end of manufacture or port of entry (for imported products) to the point of sale	*Listeria monocytogenes*	5[a]	0	100 CFU/g[b]	2[c]

Note: Where n = number of samples that must conform to the criterion; c = the maximum allowable number of defective sample units in a 2-class plan; m = a microbiological limit which, in a 2-class plan, separates acceptable lots from unacceptable lots.

[a] National governments should provide or support the provision of guidance on how samples should be collected and handled, and the degree to which compositing of samples can be employed.

[b] This criterion is based on the use of the ISO 11290-2 method. Other methods that provide equivalent sensitivity, reproducibility and reliability can be employed if they have been appropriately validated (e.g. based on ISO 16140).

[c] Assuming a log normal distribution, this sampling plan would provide 95 percent confidence that a lot of food containing a geometric mean concentration of 93.3 CFU/g and an analytical standard deviation of 0.25 log CFU/g would be detected and rejected based on any of the five samples exceeding 100 CFU/g *L. monocytogenes*. Such a lot may consist of 55 percent of the samples being below 100 CFU/g and up to 45 percent of the samples being above 100 CFU/g, whereas 0.002 percent of all the samples from this lot could be above 1 000 CFU/g. The typical actions to be taken where there is a failure to meet the above criterion would be to: (1) prevent the affected lot from being released for human consumption; (2) recall the product if it has been released for human consumption; and/or (3) determine and correct the root cause of the failure.

4.2 **Microbiological criteria for ready-to-eat foods in which growth of**
L. monocytogenes can occur

The criterion in Table 2 is intended for foods in which *L. monocytogenes* growth can occur under the conditions of storage and use that have been established for the product (see Section 3.2).

This criterion is based on the product being produced under application of the General Principles of food hygiene to the control of *L. monocytogenes* in ready-to-eat foods with appropriate evaluation of the production environment and process control (see Annex 3).

The purpose of this criterion is to provide a specified degree of confidence that *L. monocytogenes* will not be present in foods at levels that represent a risk to consumers.

Another approach can also be used (see Section 4.3).

TABLE 2

Microbiological criteria for ready-to-eat foods in which growth of _L. monocytogenes_ can occur

Point of application	Micro-organism	n	c	m	Class plan
Ready-to-eat foods from the end of manufacture or port of entry (for imported products) to the point of sale	*Listeria monocytogenes*	5[a]	0	Absence in 25 g (< 0.04 CFU/g)[b]	2[c]

[a] National governments should provide or support the provision of guidance on how samples should be collected and handled, and the degree to which compositing of samples can be employed.

[b] Absence in a 25 g analytical unit. This criterion is based on the use of ISO 11290-1 method. Other methods that provide equivalent sensitivity, reproducibility and reliability can be employed if they have been appropriately validated (e.g. based on ISO 16140).

[c] Assuming a log normal distribution, this sampling plan would provide 95 percent confidence that a lot of food containing a geometric mean concentration of 0.023 CFU/g and an analytical standard deviation of 0.25 log CFU/g would be detected and rejected if any of the five samples are positive for *L. monocytogenes*. Such a lot may consist of 55 percent of the 25 g samples being negative and up to 45 percent of the 25 g samples being positive. 0.5 percent of this lot could harbour concentrations above 0.1 CFU/g. The typical actions to be taken where there is a failure to meet the above criterion would be to: (1) prevent the affected lot from being released for human consumption; (2) recall the product if it has been released for human consumption; and/or (3) determine and correct the root cause of the failure.

4.3 **Alternative approach**

Further to the approaches described in Sections 4.1 and 4.2, competent authorities may choose to establish and implement other validated limits for the *L. monocytogenes* concentration at the point of consumption or at other points that provide an acceptable level of consumer protection for foods in which *L. monocytogenes* will not grow as well as foods in which *L. monocytogenes* growth can occur.

Owing to the large diversity among ready-to-eat food products in which growth of *L. monocytogenes* can occur, this approach would primarily be applied for specific categories or subcategories of ready-to-eat foods being produced under application of the provisions of the General Principles of food hygiene to the control of *L. monocytogenes* in ready-to-eat foods and that have a limited potential of growth over a specified shelf-life.

In establishing such limits for *L. monocytogenes*, the competent authority needs to articulate clearly the types of information required of food business operators to ensure that the hazard is controlled and to verify that these limits are achieved in practice. Information needed by competent authorities should be obtained through validation studies or other sources, and may include:

- specification for physicochemical characteristics of the products, such as pH, a_w, salt content, concentration of preservatives and the type of packaging system, taking into account the storage and processing conditions, the possibilities for contamination and the foreseen shelf-life[19] including a safety margin; and
- consultations of available scientific literature and research data regarding the growth and survival characteristics of *L. monocytogenes*.

When appropriate on the basis of the above mentioned studies, additional studies should be conducted, which may include:

- predictive mathematical modelling established for the food in question, using critical growth or survival factors for *L. monocytogenes* in the product;
- challenge tests and durability studies to evaluate the growth or survival of *L. monocytogenes* that may be present in the product during the shelf-life under reasonably foreseeable conditions of distribution, storage and use, including seasonal and regional variations.

---

[19] See footnote 2 in *Code of hygienic practice for milk and milk products* (CAC/RCP 57-2004).

ANNEX 3

RECOMMENDATIONS FOR THE USE OF MICROBIOLOGICAL TESTING FOR ENVIRONMENTAL MONITORING AND PROCESS CONTROL VERIFICATION BY COMPETENT AUTHORITIES AS A MEANS OF VERIFYING THE EFFECTIVENESS OF HACCP AND PREREQUISITE PROGRAMMES FOR CONTROL OF *LISTERIA MONOCYTOGENES* IN READY-TO-EAT FOODS

Introduction

These recommendations are for use by competent authorities if they intend to include environmental monitoring and/or process control testing as part of their regulatory activities. It is also anticipated that the Annex will provide guidance that the competent authority can provide to industry. The recommendations provide an elaboration of the concepts in Sections 5 and 6 of the main text of these Guidelines.

Guidance within Codex regarding microbiological testing is often restricted to the testing of end products using traditional lot-by-lot testing. However, the guidance provided in the main text of these Guidelines emphasizes the criticality of enhanced control of sanitation, including the appropriate use of environmental monitoring. This is further elaborated in Annex 1 "Recommendations for an environmental monitoring programme for *Listeria monocytogenes* in processing areas", which provides recommendations to industry on implementation of environmental monitoring programmes. The *Recommended International Code of Practice – General Principles of food hygiene* (CAC/RCP 1-1969) emphasizes the need to apply control measures in a systematic manner using the Hazard Analysis and Critical Control Point (HACCP) system or other food safety control systems, including the testing of in-line or finished product samples for process control verification. This Annex provides general recommendations on how competent authorities can use microbiological testing to verify the effectiveness of: (a) general hygiene programmes in the food operation environment; and (b) control measures in facilities employing HACCP or other food safety control systems.

The two types of microbiological testing programmes described below can be an important part of the ability of competent authorities to verify the effectiveness of *L. monocytogenes* control programmes over time (see Section 5.9). In developing these recommendations, no attempt is made to establish specific decision criteria for the two types of microbiological testing or the specific actions that should be taken to re-establish control. Establishment of such specific criteria and actions is more appropriately the responsibility of competent authorities owing to the diversity in products and manufacturing technologies.

a) **Environmental monitoring**

In certain instances, competent authorities may incorporate the testing of the environment (food contact and/or non-food contact surfaces) for *L. monocytogenes* (or an appropriate surrogate micro-organism [e.g. *Listeria* spp.]), as part of their regulatory requirements or activities. This can include sampling by a competent authority as part of its inspection activities or sampling performed by the individual food business operator that the competent authority can review as part of its verification of the business operator's controls (see Section 5.9). The aim of conducting and/or reviewing environmental testing programmes by a competent authority is to verify, for example, that a manufacturer has successfully identified and controlled niches and harbourage sites for *L. monocytogenes* in the food plant and to verify that sanitation programmes have been appropriately designed and implemented to control contamination by *L. monocytogenes*.

In developing environmental testing programmes and the decision criteria for actions to be taken based on the results obtained, competent authorities should clearly distinguish between sampling of food contact surfaces and non-food contact surfaces. For example, sampling locations for competent authorities may be similar to those used by food business operators (see Annex 1). In evaluating facilities that produce multiple products where at least one can support growth of *L. monocytogenes*, competent authorities should consider the importance of environmental sampling as a means of verifying that there is no cross-contamination between the products (see Section 5.2.4). In the design of an environmental verification programme, the competent authority should articulate the testing and sampling techniques that would be employed, including size, method and frequency of sampling, analytical method to be employed, locations where samples should be taken, decision criteria, and actions to be taken if a decision criterion is exceeded (similar to recommendations in Annex 1).

The competent authority should establish decision criteria that include specific conditions (e.g. specific number of positive samples) that will initiate follow-up actions (including additional testing) when an environmental sample is positive for *L. monocytogenes* or *Listeria* spp. The competent authority should also establish actions that the food business operator should anticipate if the criteria are exceeded. Detection of positive environmental samples by the competent authority exceeding the decision criteria should lead to an investigation by the food business operator and/or the competent authority to identify the source of contamination and action that should be taken by the food business operator to correct the problem. In reporting results of their analyses to food business operators, competent authorities should provide advice on the possible inferences the data provide in order to assist the food business operator in finding and correcting the source of contamination. For example, the competent authority could point out that the repeated isolation of a specific subtype of *L. monocytogenes* is indicative of a harbourage site that current sanitation activities are insufficient to control.

Overall, sampling techniques and testing methods should be sufficiently sensitive for the decision criteria established and appropriate for the surface or equipment being evaluated. Methods used should be appropriately validated for the recovery of *L. monocytogenes* from environmental samples.

b)   **Process control verification**
Business operators ensure the effectiveness of HACCP and other programmes for the control of *L. monocytogenes* in their operating facilities. Further, business operators validate the food safety control systems they have in place. Competent authorities verify that the controls are validated and being implemented as designed, through activities such as monitoring of records and activities of production personnel.

For a well-designed food safety control system, a competent authority may consider establishing microbiological process control testing and decision criteria for products to identify trends that can be corrected before decision criteria are exceeded. When undesirable trends occur or decision criteria are exceeded, the food business operator will investigate the food safety control system to determine the cause and take corrective action(s). The competent authority verifies that appropriate actions are taken when criteria are exceeded. For example, the decision criteria for process control testing could be the frequency of contamination that would be indicative of a process no longer in control and likely to produce ready-to-eat foods that do not meet the microbiological criteria established in Annex 2.

In addition to verifying that the process controls within the food safety control system are validated and operating as designed, process control testing of finished product (sometimes referred to as cross-lot or between-lot testing) has been used by business operators and/or competent authorities to detect changing patterns of contamination, which allows distinction between occasional "in control" positive samples and an emerging loss of control. Process control testing of finished product contributes to the assessment of the continuing performance of a food safety control system and helps to ensure that corrective actions are implemented before microbiological criteria are exceeded. The competent authority verifies that the food safety control system remains "in control" or ensures that the food business operator has taken corrective actions to prevent loss of control, which could include immediate corrections or changes to the food safety control system itself. The presence of *L. monocytogenes* in finished product can also indicate the lack of control of *L. monocytogenes* in the processing environment.

In certain instances, competent authorities may find it useful to establish an industry-wide process control-based criterion for *L. monocytogenes* for the purpose of ensuring that specific ready-to-eat foods undergo a consistent approach for verification of HACCP or other food safety control systems. This can include sampling by competent authorities as part of their inspection activities or sampling performed by the business operator that the competent authority can review as part of its verification of the food business operator's records.

As with other forms of verification via microbiological testing, the use of process control testing involves the establishment of decision criteria, specification of analytical methods, specification of a sampling plan, and actions to be taken in case of a loss of control. Details of process control testing principles and guidelines are beyond the scope of this Annex, but are available through standard references.